Waiting for Eddie
A Love Story

By

Albert & Karl Konrad

To the lady whose phone call + voice
changed the trajectory of my life!.

[signature]

10-24-17

AB **ASPECT Books**
www.ASPECTBooks.com

Copyright © 2017 Albert & Karl Konrad

Copyright © 2017 TEACH Services, Inc.

ISBN-13: 978-1-4796-0851-5 (Paperback)

ISBN-13: 978-1-4796-0852-2 (ePub)

ISBN-13: 978-1-4796-0853-9 (Mobi)

Library of Congress Control Number: 2017913128

Editing by Gerald Wheeler

ASPECT Books
www.ASPECTBooks.com

Table of Contents

Preface

With retirement comes time, with time comes remembrance and the need to share our family's story. We two brothers, Karl and Albert, have both passed our allotted biblical three score and ten. Time is no longer a friend in telling the story. It is time to put words on paper so that when our voices become stilled the story will not be forgotten.

It is a compelling story that begged to be written. But it was mostly talk until Albert joined Karl in full retirement in the spring of 2016. Once he was settled in his retirement he began to write and Karl joined in. Being a preacher Albert could tell a good story but it was Karl who knew the facts. He was, after all, 2 ½ years older and remembered much more of the details. They spent a week together in August of 2016 organizing the planned book.

The love story of our mom (Liese) and dad (Eddie) is one we have heard and told over the years. We boys have often talked about writing the story which began in Ukraine when Communism ruled the Soviet Union. For us boys the family's story starts in 1943 and takes our family on a perilous and tumultuous journey by train and horse-drawn wagons through Poland to Germany. It becomes the story of a single parent, who had lost her husband during WW 2, and then not knowing the language or the people, decided to come to America to start a new life for herself and her boys.

We thank the members of the Holly Seventh-day Adventist church who opened their hearts and pocketbooks to get our family settled and begin our education in America. We are also indebted to our Uncle, Willy Hann, our cousins, Paul Hann, Hans Kampen, Eduard Pabst and Stephen Kampen for their written accounts of our family's journey of faith. We appreciate the good work of our editor, Gerald Wheeler, as well as Teach Services, Inc., our publisher.

We dedicate this book to our children, grandchildren and great-grandchildren as well as to all those who encouraged us to get it down on paper. The joint writing and integration of the story has turned out to be a blessing to our own faith-journey. It is our prayer that it will be a faith-building benefit to all those who read it.

Eddie & Liese's boys,

Karl and Albert

Chapter One

A Preacher a Picture a Promise

Eddie and Liese's love story began long before they met. It all started with a brother's search, a pastor's wisdom, a picture's allure and a promise made.

Liese's brother, Willy, was a man of thought, decision and action. His mother had recently passed away, and at the age of 24 he concluded that it was high time for him to be on his own, and that meant getting married. He made it a matter of prayer. None of the local girls made his heart sing or satisfied his longing for a life time companion. In his search, he finally visited their pastor, Elder Friedrich Remfert, and asked, "Do you know any young ladies that I could meet that are not from around here?"

> *Eddie and Liese's love story began long before they met. It all started with a brother's search, a pastor's wisdom, a picture's allure and a promise made.*

The pastor didn't wait for Willy to finish his thoughts before he interjected "Willy, I thought you would never ask. I do have some possibilities for you!" He got up and went into another room to get some pictures that he carried with him of the young men and women that he had met in his travels for the church. He always carried the pictures with him for he had a burden for the church and for the young people of the church. With Stalin's vendetta against religion it was important that the youth know of others of like faith. It would enhance their ability to find a life-long and like-minded companion. So, he gladly handed him the pictures of the young women and said, "Willy, here are some nice young ladies. Look them over and choose one you want to meet."

Willy looked each picture over carefully. All the young women were fine-looking. But one appeared rather proud and another gave the impression that she wanted to be the boss of everything. And on it went until his fingers came to rest on the photo of 18-year-old Alma Konrad. He saw her smiling face and said to himself, *"This is probably the best of them all. I want to get to know her!"*

As he showed the Pastor the photo, a smile crossed the man's face. "I wondered if you would choose her. I am sure that once you get to know her you will want her to be your wife. You see if you marry her you must call me uncle for she is my niece."

That picture started a correspondence. Alma lived 1,000 kilometers from Willy's home. Her father died when she was 7. She had an older, married sister, Hilda, and a younger brother, Eddie. Her mother had married a widower and two half-sisters had joined the family: Theresa and Rosalia. Letters and more photos led to a long-distance romance. After a stint in the Russian Army, Willy made the trip to her home town. There he asked her to marry him, and she accepted. The newlyweds established their home in Khortitza where Willy lived. Economic conditions in that area were more favorable, because of the huge hydro-electric Dnieper River Dam project under construction there.

Eventually, Alma's mother, stepfather, older sister, Hilda and her husband Alexander, her younger brother, Eddie, and sister, Theresa, would also move to the area. With that the love story of Eddie and Liese slowly but surely began to come to life.

Alma, Willy, Theresa, Hilda, Eddie & Liese early in 1943.

Chapter Two
Beginnings – Liese

Liese's life started on July 10, 1910 as one of 11 children born to Henry and Katharina Hann in the Khortitza area of Ukraine. Her German ancestors had begun a journey in the early 1800's that eventually led to Ukraine from East Prussia. They came at the invitation of Russia's Catherine the Great who promised them that they would have religious freedom, local self-rule, no taxes, and most importantly, exemption from military service. The offer made in 1763 stood for decades, even after Catherine the Great's death in 1796. So, it was that a group of German settlers including those of the Hann family commenced their search to find a place of freedom and opportunity.

Liese at 24
in Khortitza, Ukraine.

For some unexplainable reason they halted near Warsaw, Poland. At the time Poland was under the protection of the Czarist government of Russia. The group found a promising portion of land near Warsaw and started a settlement of German people called Neuhof. It was here that both Liese's grandfather, Karl Edward Hann, and her father, Henry Karl Hann, were born. In Neuhof Karl Hann met and married a Mennonite (German-Dutch

Anabaptists) young woman by the name of Maria Stobe. Together they had three sons and three daughters. While Karl was Lutheran, and Maria a Mennonite, they agreed to raise their sons as Lutherans and their daughters as Mennonites.

Life in Neuhof was very difficult. Their oldest son Henry, Liese's father, born on December 3, 1864, survived babyhood but his two brothers died in infancy. He spoke often of the hard life in Poland by saying "In Poland the breadbasket hangs very high, and is unreachable for poor families." In 1889, at the age of 25, Henry decided to leave Poland and seek his fortune elsewhere. He had seen an advertisement in one of the newspapers that a Mr. Walmann from Ukraine, had a large estate farm and needed gardeners. It was just one of many enterprises that the man was involved in. He also owned a factory that produced agricultural machinery not just for the local region but for all of Russia. Deciding that here was what he had been looking for, Henry would fulfill the goal of his ancestors to go to Ukraine.

His long journey ended in Khortitza. The fact that he could speak both Russian and German impressed Mr. Walmann, and he hired Henry as chief gardener of the entire farming operation. Eventually he met a young woman by the name of Katharina Friesen, who was the head of all the female employees in the estate cafeteria. Though she was nine years younger than Henry, having been born on March 11, 1873, her beauty and good manners attracted him. She was a faithful believer in the Brethren

Liese's Father (1902)

Mennonite Church. But Henry had been raised and registered as a member of the Lutheran Church. Katharina would not marry outside of her faith and told Henry that if he wanted a good Lutheran wife he should go back home and find one. He did so and returned with not just one but two good Lutheran ladies, both of whom were his sisters. He told Katherina that he could not stop thinking about her during his journey and that in his heart she was the only one. From his mother Henry had learned what Mennonites believed and was quite willing to join Katharina's faith. It did not take long for him to study with the local pastor and become a baptized Mennonite.

In the summer of 1893 the local Mennonite pastor married Henry and Katharina. It was the custom of the day that in lieu of a honeymoon the families of the couple invited everyone to a three-day celebration. Since their parents did not live nearby, Mr. Walmann provided the place, time, and many of the gifts for the celebration. He regarded both Henry and Katharina as valued employees, essential for the successful running of the estate.

One of the gifts that Mr. Walmann gave them for their wedding was a gold-decorated German Bible. He had inscribed an admonition on the fly-leaf that said: "To my dear Henry and Katharina. If you will read this Bible daily and will live according to its words you will become the happiest and richest people in the world."

Once the celebration ended and the couple had settled into their new life together, they made good use of the special gift. Starting in Genesis, they read a portion of the Bible every day. The daily reading and study led to a major change in their beliefs and life style. It was not long before they discovered what the Bible said about what day God had designated for worship.

Their first encounter with it occurred when they read the account of Creation. "Und Gott segnete den siebenten Tag und heiligte ihn, darum daß er an demselben geruht hatte von allen seinen Werken, die Gott schuf und machte." Genesis 2:3 (Luther Bibel 1545) ("And God blessed the seventh day and declared it holy, because it was the day when he rested from all his work of creation.") New Living Translation (NLT). But it was not until they reached the 20th chapter of Exodus that they both began to wonder about just what day they should worship on.

Henry began to think about the fourth commandment and its injunction to keep the seventh-day holy. As he was tinkering in the shop after breakfast one day, he had a conversation with God. "Dear Lord," he prayed, "I see the truth of the seventh-day Sabbath, but I just got married, so please be patient with me and give me one year of peace on this matter as I need to get better acquainted with my wife. After that Lord, I promise to share this truth and my conviction with her. Please just one-year Lord. Amen." From that moment peace came to his mind and the issue did not bother him anymore.

Eventually he all but forgot his prayer, but God had not. A year later Henry was once again working in his shop when suddenly he felt a hard nudge from the side. It startled him, especially because he was alone. He looked around just to make sure that no one else was there. When he glanced at the calendar hanging on the wall, he immediately remembered the promise that he had made to the Lord about giving him peace of mind for a year. But hard as he tried he could not think of a way to keep his promise to talk to Katharina.

Finally, he left the shop and went back to the house where he silently paced back and forth in the living room. "What is the matter Henry?" Katharina asked after a while. "I have never seen you this agitated before. Have I done something to hurt you or displease you? Are you unhappy with me?"

"Oh, no sweetheart. You could never do anything like that" he exclaimed. "It is something else that we need to talk about."

"Well Henry, please tell me what it is."

So, he related the whole story of being convicted about the seventh-day Sabbath, his prayer to God, and his promise to do something once the year had passed. He described his confusion about what he read in the Bible and what their pastor always said about keeping the Ten Commandments and of Sunday being the Lord's day for worship.

"Of course, he always tells us that," she replied. "What is wrong with that?"

Henry asked her to look up the fourth commandment in the book of Exodus and read it. She did, twice, and she too was puzzled. "Gedenke des Sabbattags, daß Du ihn heiligest. Sechs Tage sollst du arbeiten und alle deine Dinge beschicken; aber am siebenten Tage ist der Sabbat des HERRN, deines Gottes." (2 Mose 20:8 Luther Bibel 1545.) ("Remember to keep the Sabbath day holy. Do all your work in six days. But the seventh day is a sabbath to honor the Lord your God." (Exodus 20:8-11, NIRV). Then they paused and prayed together about the seeming contradiction between God's Word and what they had known and practiced all their lives.

In the end, Katharina said, "Henry, if that is what the Bible says, then we must do it. So, let's continue to study. Maybe we will find more information on this later." It pleased Henry that his wife had such an open heart and mind, and together they covenanted that they would accept whatever the Bible taught and live accordingly. So as to not disturb the church and their friends, they decided they would keep the Sabbath holy at home and on Sunday they would go to church. By doing that they thought they would be in full harmony with the Bible and at peace with their neighbors.

Small tightly-knit communities do not keep secrets well, neither do they tolerate life-altering differences. It was not long before the neighbors wondered why they did not see the couple "around and about" on Saturdays doing their normal chores. One Saturday they decided to check up on them, and when they came to their home they saw that the whole family was neatly dressed and studying the Bible. "We came because we were worried but we see that all is well. How come you are all dressed up? This isn't Sunday."

Henry explained to them why they were not in their working clothes. He tried to show them from the Bible what it said about the Sabbath, but they were not interested. They went straight to the pastor to inform him about the heresy that they had just uncovered.

That led to further conversations and eventual excommunication from the local congregation, because of "heretical Jewish beliefs." The pastor informed Henry's boss that something needed to be done. Mr. Walmann visited and tried his best to dissuade them both from their supposed heretical teaching. When he saw that his efforts were fruitless he, said, "Henry, I, myself, don't understand what you believe and why you are prac-

Small tightly-knit communities do not keep secrets well, neither do they tolerate life-altering differences.

ticing Saturday worship, but you are one of my very best employees, and I need you here on the estate. You can't work on Saturday and I can't let you work on Sunday so you must complete the necessary tasks in five days." Both Henry and Katharina were able to continue to work for some time under this arrangement.

After continued harassment from their former pastor and several of the church members, they both decided it was time to leave the estate. Moving to the next settlement, Nikolaipol, Henry struck out on his own. There he earned a living as a gardener and security guard for area farmers. He watched their field and gardens for predators and fires by night and grew fruits and vegetables to sell by day. The income allowed him both to care for his family and to save enough money to build his first house for their ever-growing family. From the time of their marriage till about 1910 eleven children were born, seven boys and four girls. Unfortunately two of the boys and one girl died in their infancy.

Even in their new home and work they both felt the sting of the isolation that their new-found belief in the seventh-day Sabbath brought. Unaware of any other individuals who worshipped as they did, they prayed that God would strengthen their belief and help them find others who shared it.

One Friday afternoon a man driving a horse drawn wagon stopped at the house and introduced himself: "Hello, I am Mr. Schlagel and I am selling religious books and need a place to stay for the weekend. Would you folks have an extra room or bed that I could rent?" They agreed to give him room and refused any money. Glad for the change of pace that visitors brought, most people during those days would share their accommodations free of charge.

Schlagel unhitched his horse and entered the house. Since it was Friday afternoon, Katharina was in full preparation for the coming Sabbath. Surprised by her activity, he asked, "Isn't today Friday? Folks don't usually spend their time cleaning the house and getting ready for church on Friday. They do that on Saturday. Why are you cleaning today?"

Quickly Katharina explained that though they were believers in Christ they were getting ready for worship on His Sabbath day.

The man then introduced himself as a fellow Sabbath keeper and that he represented scores of other Sabbath observers in Russia. He was an American pastor of the Seventh-day Adventist Church who had come to Russia to distribute literature to the German-speaking villages in the area surrounding Khortitza. It thrilled Henry and Katharina to learn that many others also honored the seventh-day Sabbath. They were not alone in their faith and practice. After further study and baptism, they became members of the Seventh-day Adventist church and eventually participated in the establishment of the first Adventist congregation in the area.

During the early 1900's prejudice once again raised its ugly head in Nikolaipol, and they moved back to Khortitza. Initially Henry went back to work for Mr. Walmann as the chief purchaser of breeding cattle for the estate farm. This was the family's final move it would be there that most of their children would grow up.

Now began a period of relative prosperity broken by the ravages of World War I (1914–1918) and then the Russian Civil War (1917–1921). Both events interrupted the lives of Khortitza's residents. The civil war raged on in frightening ferocity until Lenin and the Communists got the upper hand and were in power. Things were chaotic in Ukraine during this period of constant upheaval.

The various factions of the civil war targeted the Mennonite colonies, because they were far better off than the regular Ukrainian peasants. Marauders invaded the Mennonite homes, murdered, raped at will, and spread various diseases until most of the local population contracted typhoid fever and many died. The famine, pestilence and violence of the times also severely affected the Hann family. On Christmas Eve in 1919 Henry finally succumbed to typhoid fever and passed away. As his life ebbed slowly away his family could hear him in prayer: "Unser Vater in dem Himmel! Dein Name werde geheiligt." Matthew 6:9 (Luther Bibel 1545). ("Father in heaven, Hallowed be Your name," NKJV). To the very end he expressed his faith and trust in the Lord to care for him. Liese also contracted typhoid and was expected to die. In fact, they saved the left-over lumber from her dad's coffin to be used for hers. But as was often the case when Liese was involved, God had not spoken His word yet. By His Grace Liese survived and lived another 63 years.

Henry's death left Katharina alone to care for her children, ranging from Katie, the oldest at 24, to Liese as the youngest, at 9. She ended up having to count on her second eldest son, Henry, to lead the family. The army had drafted her oldest son, Eric, and sent him off to Turkey, and Else had married in 1918. During the intervening years 6 of the 8 living children found companions and married. Willy, the youngest of the boys, was married in 1932. That left two of the children, Gerhard and Liese, both single, to care for Katharina. The passing years were anything but kind for her. Finally, on May 4 in 1932 she could fight no more, and her body gave out. The children took her to be buried near her beloved Henry. Liese and Gerhard remained single longer than any of their siblings. She kept house and worked on the collective farm as a store keeper.

People wondered about Liese's inability to find the right man to marry her. They gossiped that perhaps she was meant to be a spinster. For Liese, it was not that she wanted to be alone all her life, but rather she intended to make sure that she found the right man to spend her life with.

Liese and her brother, Gerhard in front of the Family Home in 1935.

Chapter Three

Beginnings – Eddie

*Eddie at 18
in Khortitza, Ukraine.*

Eddie's life began on June 17, 1918 as the third of four children born to Wilhelm Konrad and his wife Mathilde (nee Remfert) Konrad. Eddie's two sisters, Hilda and Alma, and a younger brother, Friedrich completed the family. His father, Wilhelm, initially worked on a farm owned by a Seventh-day Adventist pastor/farmer, Karl Friedrich Remfert. Wilhelm quickly fell in love with the farmer's oldest daughter, Mathilde, and they married. The Remfert farm was near the small city of Blumenthal located in in Zhytomyr county, Volhynia province, in the northwest corner of Ukraine, bordering Poland to the west and Belarus to the north. During the mid-1800s many Germans had settled in Volhynia.

Shortly after Eddie's birth his dad entered the Adventist ministry full time and in the early 1920's the denomination transferred him east to the Volga German Autonomous Soviet Socialist Republic where he provided care and nurture to Adventist church members living in that area.

Not long after their arrival, the region experienced severe famine and starvation. The famine began in the early spring of 1921 and lasted through 1922 resulting in the deaths of an estimated 6 million people. The economic disturbances caused by WW1, the Russian Civil War, rail networks that could not distribute food effectively, as well as the lack of rain all combined to exacerbate the intensity of the famine. It became a national catastrophe affecting most of the grain-growing regions.

Eddie's grandfather heard about the terrible conditions and invited the family to come back home. In contrast to the rest of Russia, their region had experienced a bountiful harvest. Not only was there plenty of food but also room for all of them on the family farm. He was willing to give his son-in-law land on which to build a house. The invitation was God-sent as it would allow Eddie's father to continue his pastoral work for the church members who lived near the homestead.

Making the decision to return home, the family purchased tickets and quickly boarded the train, eager to get on the way. What should have been a journey of just a few days turned into a trail of tears and death. The difficulties of the post-revolution times, uncertain train schedules and spreading famine, caused the journey to take over two months. Their food supplies ran out and there was very little available for purchase. Typhoid fever ran rampant throughout the train. No one seemed to be immune from it. When the train stopped at Kiev, Eddie's dad succumbed to the scourge and died. Along with scores of others who had died, he was carried off and buried outside of the city in a mass grave.

All alone, with no husband, and four children to care for, 250 kilometers from home, and no way to contact her parents about the situation, Mathilde had to decide by herself how to proceed. The station master informed her that the nearest depot for Blumenthal was in the city of Zhytomyr. They arrived at that station, it was the middle of winter, the children sick, and still forty kilometers from home. Things seemed so grim that Mathilde felt hopeless. Her husband had always taken

Eddie's Father (1918)

care of situations such as this. Here she was, in dire straits, without his strength and experience, but she believed that God would sustain them.

In desperation, she bowed her head and prayed. After concluding her prayer, she noticed an elderly man driving by her family in a one-horse wagon. When she spoke to him, he answered her in German. "I am all alone here with four very sick children," she explained, "and I need to get to my parent's farm as quickly as possible. My father will pay you once we reach there. Will you take us?" Moved with compassion, the man agreed to drive them the 40 kilometers.

After several very cold hours of riding in the wagon they all finally arrived at her father's farm. As her dad came out to greet them he saw how emaciated, hungry, and frozen they all appeared. Quickly he hurried them into the house. After paying the kind man, he turned his attention to his daughter and grandchildren. Although the tender care of her parents brought comfort and healing to Mathilde and her children, they would have to endure one more sorrow. The youngest of the children, Friedrich, had suffered far too much for his little body to heal, and he succumbed to the ravages of the typhoid fever.

Eddie's grandfather subdivided his large farm among his seven living children so that each family had a house and a modest acreage. Mathilde's brothers helped work her land.

Before long the joy of being with family eased the sorrow of the past. For Mathilde and her children life took on a routine of normalcy. The oldest sister, Hilda, met a young man, Alexander Pabst, who attended the same Adventist church as they did. It was not long until she married him.

He invited his parents to live with them since life in the Volga region was so difficult. Travel in those days was hazardous, and on the way Alexander's mother died and was buried near Kiev. His father, Solomon, and the children continued their journey and settled near Eddie's family.

Since Eddie's mother needed help in running her portion of the farm, she hired Solomon Pabst. Proving to be more than a good worker, he fell in love with Mathilde. They soon married and sought to blend their two families. Eventually they added two little girls to it, Theresa and Rosalia.

Try as he might, Eddie just could not establish a close relationship with his stepfather. Solomon was a good man and did not mistreat him. It was simply that Solomon was not his birth father and never would be. He had a closer relationship with his grandfather than he had with his newly acquired stepfather. As Eddie entered his teenage years, his older sister, Hilda, and her husband, Alexander, who was an excellent photographer, decided to move some 3,000 kilometers away to the city of Tbilisi in the Republic of Georgia to start a photography studio. The choice was a logical decision since the winters were much milder and German settlers lived in the area.

In the beginning things went quite well, and Alexander suggested that the Pabst family join them. When Eddie was 14 years old his mom and stepfather also decided to move to Tbilisi in the hopes of a better life. The boy did not want to move but had no choice in the matter. Alma, his one remaining sister, had decided not to move because she was soon going to marry her fiancé, Willy Hann. Willy's home was in Khortitza, in southcentral Ukraine where a great hydro-electric dam was in process of completion and had created a great deal of economic activity.

In Tbilisi, the climate was great but economic conditions were not. Circumstances deteriorated. Decent places to live were way too expensive, Solomon could not find good work, and Alexander's photography business dried up. The families tried their best to make a go of it, but things just kept getting worse. It got so bad that it was difficult for Solomon to provide enough food for the three children let alone for himself and Eddie's mom.

Alexander suggested that they move to Zaporozhe, a Ukrainian city across the Dnieper River from Khortitza where Willie and Alma lived. When the pastor of the Tbilisi Adventist Church heard of their impending move to Ukraine, he and his wife approached Eddies stepfather and mother with an unusual proposition. "We have tried to have children of our own but can't, so would you let us adopt one of Eddie's little sisters. We will give her the very best of everything that we can afford. She will want nothing. We will love her as if she were our very own." The suggestion appalled Eddie, and his mother simply said, "No!" But as their living conditions continued to deteriorate, she finally agreed with her husband that the only right thing to do was to allow the younger of the two girls, Rosalia, to be adopted. At the time Rosalia was 5 years old and Eddie was 15. Neither was old enough to stop the adoption process.

*Eddie's mom, Eddie, Theresa
and his stepfather Solomon 1935.*

When the pastor and his wife came to pick her up, Rosalia screamed, "Please, mamma, don't make me go. Please let me stay with you. I love you and don't want to go." The heart-wrenching scene forever etched itself in Eddie's heart. But she was made to go. The family then made the move to Khortitza. With the loss of Rosalia, Mathilde was never the same again and died in 1936. With her death, the family disintegrated. Eddie and Theresa, made their home with either Alma or Hilda. Alexander finding a good job in a photography shop, taught Eddie the trade and both worked there for several years.

His approaching adulthood and the ability to be self-supporting highlighted his need for a place to call his own.

Turning out to be an excellent photographer, Eddie was so successful that in later years he could help others financially. He also became proficient in tailoring. When one of Liese's nephews, Hans Kampen, graduated from a teacher-training course, Eddie made him a pair of trousers so that he could teach in style.

Eddie developed a close relationship with his brother-in-law, Willie, who was 10 years older. He admired Willie's maturity, abilities and drive. One result of his relationship with Willie and Alma in Khortitza was that he became acquainted with the Hann family, as well as other Adventist families and their young people. It was here when he felt the need of a place and family to call his own that he met Liese. His approaching adulthood and the ability to be self-supporting highlighted his need for a place to call his own.

Chapter Four

Life Together

Raised in a Seventh-day Adventist home, with a grandfather, father, and uncles who were ministers in that faith, he was certainly partial to the faith but had not yet made his full commitment to it by being baptized. In his association with the young people Eddie became acquainted with several of the young women. He got to know one of them well; Liese (Elisabeth) Hann, his brother-in-law, Willie's younger unmarried sister. Eight years older than Eddie, well into her twenties, she was considered somewhat of an "old maid" since most young women usually married by their late teens or early twenties.

Eddie & Liese shortly after their wedding in 1937.

Liese had good reasons why she was still single. As the youngest of the family, she was the one called upon to be the caregiver whenever it needed one. Baptized at 14 and dedicated to her faith, she worked as a clerk at the local collective store. Her cheerful, sensible, and steady spiritual outlook, when compared to his own tumultuous family life, drew him to her.

Furthermore, she was an excellent cook and an experienced house-keeper. As they became better acquainted, Liese noted his strengths, saw that they balanced each other, and she fell in love with him. Eddie and Liese both had lost their parents while relatively young and were now on their own.

At 18 he proposed and she, at 27, accepted. Liese's older and still single brother, Gerhard, had found his own Liese (Kohn) and the couples planned a double wedding for December 30, 1937. At first both couples lived in what had been mother Hann's home. Because of the small space it was easy to get in each other's way, and soon Eddie and Liese made the move to their own apartment.

It didn't take long before they expected the birth of their first child. A baby girl, Klara, was born. Their happiness, however, was short lived. Klara developed medical problems and died at age six weeks, devastating her parents. The death was so sudden, so unexpected. Where was God they wondered? Why did she have to dies so young? Some in the church suggested that God couldn't answer their prayers, because Eddie was not fully committed to the faith. Such an attitude made the couple's sorrow even more bitter. Her siblings, however, reminded her that the death of infants was not uncommon. They and their own mother had lost babies and children to illness.

In spite of the sorrow life moved on. Eddie established himself as a photographer and earned a good living. The massive dam project engen-dered much economic activity. New people moved into the area, and the Communist Government required photo ID's for the many documents they had to have. Most of his clients also wanted extra pictures. On weekends people crowded the river beaches to relax and afterward stopped by the shop to have themselves photographed. On Sunday Eddie, would take the photographs and Liese would keep

One of Eddie's photos developed at his shop in 1942.

the records. The photos were always ready on the following Sunday and greatly supplemented his income.

At times Eddie's generous heart frustrated Liese. He was willing to help whoever asked him for assistance, and by the time he arrived home from his photography studio the extra money he had earned had mostly gone to relatives and friends in need. With what was left Liese had to manage the household expenses as well as to save some. Eddie loved company and would often invite hungry students home for a meal. Meeting one of his friends he would ask, "How are things going?"

Most of the times the answer would be, "Not so great, I am having a tough time right now. My student stipend is late and I haven't eaten since yesterday."

The winds of war had beaten the flames of trouble into an inferno.

"Well, you must come home with me. My wife, Liese, is a great cook and she's been shopping today." So, Eddie would arrive home with one or more of his friends in tow.

Shopping seemed easy to Eddie for he never had to do it. But for Liese it was a real chore. No matter where she went, she always encountered long waiting lines. She carefully planned her menus and made lists so that grocery staples would last for several days. Since cold storage for perishables was not available, she had to purchase them daily. With the unexpected company Liese had to shop more frequently. Advancing pregnancy now made being on her feet for several hours each day more and more wearying. But, Eddie was happy and so was she, and that was what mattered.

On February 18, 1941, a son was born and they named him Karli (diminutive for Karl). Less than four months later Nazi Germany invaded the Soviet Union. And with the invasion uncertainty once again swept into their lives. The "Blitzkrieg" style of warfare moved so rapidly that before one could fully grasp the meaning of the invasion, it was over. The winds of war had beaten the flames of trouble into an inferno.

Prior to the invasion the Soviet government had intended to deport all residents of German descent from Ukraine to the eastern republics of Russia, but the German Wehrmacht advanced so quickly that Soviet officials could not execute the plan. At first both the German colonists and the Ukrainians hailed the occupation as an act of emancipation. But the ill-treatment of the Ukrainian population by the Germans soon made the local non-Germans detest them and seek to undermine their control.

Liese and Karli 1941 in Khortitza.

The invaders gave all German speaking men living in the occupied territory the choice of either joining the German Wehrmacht (Army) or being conscripted for service to whatever branch of the various services that at the time needed men. Eddie decided that he would join the Wehrmacht before he was drafted, basing his decision, first, on the reality of the situation as the Germans occupied all of Ukraine. Second, on the memories of the persecution and death of his grandfather, two uncles and one brother-in-law by the Communists for their Christian faith and leadership. And finally, on the reality of being German and not Russian. So, he told Liese, "If I join then, I have a choice and will not be forced to serve in the SS. I believe they will recognize my fluency in both German and Russian and allow me to serve as a translator for their interrogation services."

(The Nazi Party established the Waffen-SS, translated as Armed Protection Squad, as its armed wing. During the war it grew from three regiments to over 38 divisions and eventually included not only men from Nazi Germany, but also volunteers and conscripts from both occupied and un-occupied lands. They actually served as the spearhead of the German advance and served alongside the regular army but were never formally part of it.)

"Eddie, you know I detest violence and war," she replied. "I wish that you wouldn't have to do this. I will pray that God will bless your decision, keep you safe, and that you might continue to be stationed near us." His decision initially worked out just as he had hoped and Liese had prayed for.

Eddie ended up near the war front, serving as an interpreter during prisoner interrogations. It was not long before Russian bombers penetrated the German lines and flew over the Khortitza area dropping bombs indiscriminately. Liese would have to pick up Karli and run to the nearest bomb shelter. Racing down the stairs into the shelter kept them safe from the air raids but they were painful for Liese. To keep Karli safe, she often stumbled down the stairs and in the process, broke several of her ribs. Unable to get medical attention the breaks healed on their own and plagued her the remainder of her life. But she had kept her little boy safe, and that was what mattered most.

Eddie in his German Army uniform 1944.

Chapter Five

Journey and Separation

Karli had been born in the local hospital at the beginning of 1941 and in relative tranquility prior to the German occupation of Khortitza. Liese's second son, Albi (diminutive for Albert), was born September 22, 1943 just as events began to turn against the German army.

Their lightning advances now turned into stalemate and finally retreat. The hospital was no longer available as it had become a barracks for the German soldiers. An officer of the German occupying forces had taken over the house as his quarters so Albi was born in one of the out buildings on the property.

The push back by the Soviet Army grew stronger each passing day and eventually it was as swift as the German invasion had been. Eight days after Albi's birth, the family found itself evacuated west to Poland. Since no regular coach-type railroad cars were available for the hurriedly arranged exodus, the German authorities loaded the family along with many other ethnic Germans into box cars and sent them to a resettlement camp located in an area still under firm German military control.

More than 300,000 ethnic Germans from Ukraine were able to escape to Poland before the Russian Army seized thousands of other German refugees attempting to flee. With few exceptions, the former residents of Khortitza were deported to Siberia and Kazakhstan. There the Soviets simply released them on the bare land to fend for themselves as best as they could. Many did not survive.

The trip to Poland lasted 11 days and nights. Often the train could only proceed in darkness, because of the frequent daytime air raids. But nights were just as dangerous as Polish partisans sought to wreak havoc on German rail traffic, since it carried not only civilians for resettlement but also troops and armaments. Fortunately, the weather remained relatively warm and sunny until they arrived at the Main Integration Office in Pre-usisch-Stargard, Poland.

The train made a rest stop on the way to Poland during October 1943.

The city and the refugee camps there served as the equivalent of "Ellis Island" for all of Europe's ethnic Germans. The main purpose of the screening was to ensure the purity of their German ancestry. At the time, the Nazi authorities classified all Germans into three basic categories. Eddie, Liese and all their family members were "Volksdeutsche," a term meaning "German-folk." It referred to ethnic Germans living outside of Germany and who had not been born in Germany proper but who were considered eligible for German citizenship. The prime designation was that of "Reichsdeutsche" ("Imperial Germans"). They were Germans who had been born and lived within Germany's borders. The third group were the "Auslandsdeutsche" ("Foreign Germans"), people of German citizenship permanently residing in other countries. Liese's extended family spent the next nine months in the resettlement camp called "Conradstein."

She and all her brothers and sisters received German passports and were full-fledged citizens. Eddie had gained his passport upon being inducted into the Wehrmacht.

It was in this camp that Karli and his two-year older cousin, Eddie Pabst, having had enough of war decided to find where heaven was and go there. They had been taught that in heaven there would be no more war, pain, suffering, and that they would have all the food they ever wanted. They had also listened to the story of Enoch, who in the Old Testament walked with God until he walked right into heaven. Concluding, as only two little boys could, that what worked for Enoch might just do the same for them. They decided to run away toward where the sky and the earth met. After all, that is where heaven should be! It did not seem that far, and the road out of camp led straight to that spot. So off they went to find heaven. But they had not gone very far when one of the men from the camp, as he drove along in a truck, saw them by the side of the road. Recognizing them he offered them a ride. Karli and Eddie accepted and before they realized what was happening, they found themselves back in the camp and safe in the arms of their worried mothers.

While Karli took to camp life and was not affected by the unhealthy living conditions in the camp, Albi had a difficult time and hovered between life and death. Liese just could not produce enough breast milk to provide him adequate nourishment. Although taken to the camp nursery, his condition did not improve. Eddie's sister, Theresa, spent most of her days as well as nights with Albi at the nursery making sure no one kidnapped the little boy. Everyone was worried about what they could do to get nourishment into his body. Finally, his Tante (Aunt) Else, told Liese, "Just give that little boy some sugar. You can dilute it with regular milk and I am sure he will drink it all up. It can't hurt, can it? The nurses think he is going to die anyway." His mother decided to try it, and Albi took to it like bees to honey. It was not long until he was gaining weight. Soon he became a happy and healthy baby and the nursery released him to go back to Liese's arms.

While the nurses thought Albi might be adorable, they were totally smitten by Karli's deep blue eyes and tow-headed blonde hair. When he spent time there with his Tante (Aunt) Theresa watching over his little brother, the nurses would give him a biscuit and a cup of hot milk. Delicious! To Liese the boys were adorable and handsome when they slept but generally quite a handful when they were awake.

By the summer of 1944 all of Liese's family had been assigned housing in the village of Lask in central Poland. What none of them knew or suspected at the time was that it had been a center for Jewish life before the German occupation. Historical documents show that prior to 1939, 3,864 Jews (68 percent of a total population of 6,000 people) had lived in Lask. All the resident population of Jewish descent had been removed from Lask and deported either to a labor camp or a concentration camp. The housing the refugees received had probably once belonged to Jewish families.

The Barracks were Liese and her family were housed 1943–44.

Since Eddie's enlistment and induction during fall of 1941 the army had not granted him a proper leave. Because his translating services had been in great demand and always kept him at the battle front, the military authorities had allowed him only a few short breaks. Now the Wehrmacht was in retreat mode and was not taking many prisoners. In late 1944 he received a lengthy furlough to make winter preparations for his family. He was able to spend part of December and the first part of January with Liese and the boys while his unit was being reorganized. He even made a wooden sled with a removable seat back. Real winter weather had set in and hard-packed snow covered the streets. He bundled up the boys, sat Karli on the sled, braced him against the seat back, placed Albi on his lap and wrapped them in a blanket, then pulled them up and down the streets. He set a fast pace and the boys shrieked with delight. It was great to be doing something peaceful.

Eddie had time to look at his sleeping boys and process his military experiences. Kept safe while others near him had been killed, he had worked to make it easier for the POWs and never had to shoot an enemy.

Once his superiors had ordered Eddie to take a dangerous prisoner to the lockup. The officer in charge told him the man was dangerous and would probably attempt escape. In that case, Eddie's orders were to shoot to kill. The felon did make a break and Eddie pulled the trigger. Inexplicably, the Luger service revolver jammed and the man escaped. Eddie wondered what connection Liese's prayers had with all he'd been through.

Eddie, Albi, Liese and Karli in late 1944.

His marriage to Liese and observing her steady faith made him rethink his attitude toward God. Now he had time to attend church services and reflect on his spiritual roots. Eddie began an intense study of the teachings of the church with his brother-in-law, Willy. Although convicted to make his peace with God and fully join the faith that his dad and grandfather had preached and taught, he was unable to follow through on his decision to be baptized. It was winter and there were no facilities or an ordained minister available.

Eventually Eddie received orders to report for active duty in Posen (Poznan) by January 15, 1945. With a heavy heart, he prepared to leave. "Liese," he said, "I have done all I could to get coal and wood for heat and cooking stacked in the back entry. You have grocery staples and ration cards. It is enough to see you through the winter. I am leaving you my two woolen Wehrmacht blankets and my canteen." He realized and feared that because of the unpredictable war situation the family might have to leave Lask before winter ended. Hugging and kissing them all once more, he prayed, "Oh God watch over my family!" Then turning and shutting the door, he walked to his transport.

It soon became apparent that the Russians were advancing west at an alarming rate. The regional military authority had concluded that the Russia Army was moving so quickly that it was necessary to relocate all the children and young adults to a safer area. They decided to load all of them immediately on all available trucks. Liese, Theresa, Karli and Albi daily went to the train station to check on available transportation out of the city as well as any information of troop movements that might indicate if and when Eddie would be in the area. As they stood in line for information Liese found it necessary to leave Karli with Theresa as she went to the ticket agent's window. Just at that moment the authorities began to enforce the evacuation order for the children and soldiers began to place them on the trucks.

With Liese gone, 17-year-old Theresa did not have the presence of mind to act quickly as soldiers grabbed Karli and heaved him up on the truck that would be leaving as soon as it was full. Karli was sitting on the edge of the truck bed and the driver was revving up the motor when Liese returned and saw what was about to happen. Instantly, with Theresa's help, she pulled him off the truck before anyone could stop her. The soldiers were only there to carry out their orders, which were meant to protect children and keep them out of danger. But Liese knew that separation no matter how well-intentioned and planned could be permanent in the chaotic nature of war. Shaken by the close call, she returned to the house to plan her next move.

Theresa was scheduled to leave shortly for Friedensau in eastern Germany. The government had confiscated and closed the Adventist school there but had allowed the home for seniors to continue operating. The authorities considered Theresa mature enough to contribute to the war effort by caring for the elderly.

The fighting between the Germans and Russians was so intense and close that Liese could hear the cannons and see the planes in the air preparing to drop their deadly bombs. Her brother Willy came from next door and told Liese that it was time to pack up and leave. She along with her two sisters, Else and Tina, protested. They insisted that they were staying and waiting for their loved ones who were in the German Army. The sisters had four sons who had been conscripted for Army duty and Liese of course had her Eddie in the army. But Willy insisted and finally persuaded all three to get their

His marriage to Liese and observing her steady faith made him rethink his attitude toward God.

winter coats and take whatever they could carry to their bother Gerhard's place. Once they were there they all together would determine what to do and where to go. Liese loaded Karli on to the little sled that Eddie had made, placed Albi on his lap, and pulled them as they hurriedly walked toward Gerhard's place.

Along the way they saw a young woman standing beside a small horse and wagon, looking forlorn and lost. Willy asked if he could be of any help. "Can you please help me get the wagon and the horse onto the main street?" she asked.

"You can't do that because the street is jammed with wagons and tanks," he replied. "By the way, which way are you trying to go?"

"I need to go downtown to pick up my parents." Then glancing down the street in the direction that she needed to go, she saw the impossibility of getting through. Quickly she headed back to the wagon, picked up her suitcase, and started to walk away. As she left she yelled back to Willy, "Do whatever you want with that horse and wagon."

He looked at the number of family members traveling with him and decided that he would take the horse and wagon. A small wagon would be of real help in dealing with all the children. Since he was traveling in the direction of the traffic flow he could quickly get the wagon in line and head to Gerhardt's house. By the time they reached it the total number of their group had grown to 28. There were just two adult men and the rest were women and children with the youngest being only nine months old. With the wagon Willy realized that they would be able to take more of the luggage that they had left behind, so he and Gerhardt decided to go back to his house and get it. By staying off the main road they were able to move quickly and retrieve the needed suitcases.

On the way back they saw a Polish man trying to get his horses to pull forward and head to the center of the city. But the animals would not move even when he lashed them with his whip. Willy stopped and asked him what he was doing and why was he so violent with the horses. "I have to go downtown to pick up my boss's furniture and take it to Germany," he shouted. "My boss left yesterday."

Looking directly at him, Willy said, "Sir, if you leave Poland today you will never see your family again!"

"I know that, but what can I do?"

"Look," Willy suggested, "here is what you can do. Give me the horses and the wagon and hide yourself and your family till the Russians come. You are Polish and will be safe with them unlike us Germans. And if I have the wagon I and my family will be able to escape before the Russians catch us." The man jumped down from the wagon, gave Willy the reins and disappeared into the crowd.

Now the problem was, how to get the horses and the wagon back to where all the family waited. Willy was not in the habit of using a whip on horses, but in this case he made an exception. Pulling the reins tight, he applied the whip as gently as he could, and the horses began to head into the busy street. As they moved forward Gerhardt and Willy yelled at the top of their voices, "Wild horses! Wild horses! Get out of the way! Get out of the way! We can't control them!" The people in the street parted rather quickly, opening a path for the horses. In short order, they arrived safely at Gerhardt's place. Quickly everyone and their belongings got on the two wagons and fled.

Several kilometers out of the city Liese glanced back at where they had come from. All she could see was the orange glow of fires and the ruins of a town that she had not wanted to leave. Surely, she thought, God was with Willy when he urged her to accompany him. Her prayer was not only for herself and her boys but also for her Eddie. She would have to leave his care to God. The story of their lives together began as an affair of the heart, but war, distance, and time were turning it into a tragedy of separation.

In the turmoil of the flight Liese along with her brothers lost all sense of direction. The group had no map and were unprepared for the long journey that stretched before them. Their only choice was to follow the rest of the mass of refugees. Often they traveled on back roads, but always checking to make sure either by the direction of sunlight or moonlight that they were heading in a westerly direction. The journey lasted more than two months and 1,000 kilometers.

Trying to keep Albi and Karli warm and fed proved to be an enormous task. Albi was not the youngest of the group at almost 1 ½ years old. His cousin, Anni, was just six months old. Somehow, amazingly, God provided just enough food and warmth to keep everyone in the group from starving, freezing or even getting frostbite.

When they traveled on the better roads so many other refugees crowded them that it was almost impossible to make any progress. Liese's brother kept looking for an alternate route that was also going in a westerly direction. When he had all but given up hope he saw a road ahead that was less traveled but seemed to be heading in the right direction. He decided to take this road as he felt he could make better time and get ahead of the mob. While he had no idea what lay ahead, he felt that there was no other choice.

Willy knew he had to keep going. Stopping was not an option.

Soon it became dusk. The road went through a valley with mountains on one side and dense forest on the other, leaving no room to turn around. Willy knew he had to keep going. Stopping was not an option. They passed groups of armed men and women resting on the sides of the road. Listening to their conversations, Liese soon realized that they were not speaking German but Polish. From the gist of their conversations they were partisans who were seeking members of the German army and others to capture. Willy did not even stop to offer a prayer seeking God's help. Everyone prayed silently and continually. As Willy was deep in prayer one of the boys crawled up to him and whispered; "Uncle Willy, Uncle Willy, look back, there are two riders on horses coming from behind us at full speed!"

Seeing the two riders driving their horses at a furious pace Willy feared that it might be the end of their journey. He thought that the soldiers would force the group to follow them, turning them over to the Russians. As the riders reached the back of the wagons, they parted to each side. When they got to the front of the wagons neither rider said a word. They simply pointed at Willy and motioned him to follow. It was the only option. The soldiers on the horses still remained silent. After accompanying them out of that dangerous valley, the riders turned to the right and raced away as quickly as they had come, leaving the refugees alone on a clear road that led directly to the next town. Quietly they all thanked God for answering their prayers.

That town, like many other villages and towns on the route, proved to be almost empty. Fearing the advancing Russian Army moving relentlessly westward, its citizens had fled. The refugees were always on the lookout for food and feed for the horses. One of the boys called out, "Uncle Willy, look there is a pile of oats and hay." Stopping to let the horses eat and rest they loaded as much of the hay and oats as they could. The hay proved to be a double blessing as it not only fed the horses but kept the children warm when they covered themselves with it.

The women and children were so thankful for the horse feed that they began to sing hymns of praise. Before long the singing attracted others on the road and they too joined their voices in praise. Total strangers became friends as the words and melodies of the hymns bound them together. Everyone, family or stranger, stopped long enough to offer prayer and praise to God for His leading and care. One happy day they were offered another small black horse. What a boon for Gerhardt. The small horses worked well together, had a lot of stamina and could keep up with Willy's team.

Fear of the advancing Russian Army forced the group to let the horses travel as fast and as long as they could. Turmoil and panic engulfed the group with the sound of gun fire, obscene screaming, cursing, and people scurrying without thought of direction or purpose. The only thing that could be done was to keep moving westward. To change direction or linger meant risking the lives of the children and grownups. Regardless of the weather and weariness, they had to press onward until they were away from the onslaught of the Red Army.

Some days later they were traveling alone and evening was coming on. Passing through a forest when ahead of them they noticed a large compound with a three-story house. Willy pointed the horses in its direction. As the group entered the gates to the farm compound they saw several German soldiers standing at the ready with their machine guns. But the men made no effort to stop the wagons. Noticing a flickering light coming from the basement door, Willy walked toward it and stepped inside. He found a warm fire and food cooking on the stove.

Quickly all the women and children were inside the basement trying to get warm. *Finally a warm place and good food,* Liese thought. But before anyone could get comfortable, an officer stepped forward and barked out, "All civilians must leave immediately. This place is only for the area's Commanding General and his soldiers! Leave immediately or risk being shot!" With the command echoing in their ears, everyone reluctantly left the warm kitchen as quickly as they had come in. As they walked back to the wagons Liese and the others silently prayed that God would do something to help them. The children just could not go another night without heat and hot food.

Though deep in silent prayer they could hear a man's voice talking directly to them. He looked at Willy and said "Follow me. I will show you where you can stay tonight." They trudged behind him to another building on the compound, it had a staircase on the outside leading to the upper floor. Making his way up the staircase and opening the door, he directed them to accompany him. Everyone went inside to a large heated room occupied by soldiers.

The man who had taken them up the stairs now ordered all the soldiers to vacate the premises. The room would serve for other purposes that night. The oldest of the billeted soldiers protested, "I am not leaving. Nobody is going to give me orders tonight." Their guide walked over to him and said simply, "Soldier, you had better obey if you know what is good for you!" Without hesitation, the soldier picked up his gear and headed to the door along with all the others in the room. Liese had thought that there was going to be a fight for their host's uniform was that of an ordinary private in the German Army. But his voice carried an authority beyond his status and all ended well. She did not know what to make of it all but the warmth was beckoning. "Don't be upset," he announced. "Everything is going to be fine, for I have the authority to do all this. First, I am going to order a hot meal for all of you, and then I will see to it that your horses are fed and stabled for the night. You are under my protection, so get some rest." It was not long until someone brought food upstairs, and when they finished eating, they were all able to sleep without any disturbance.

The next morning they heard a knock on the door. It was the friendly soldier who now asked how everyone had slept. "We all slept well and are warm and rested," Willy said.

> *"…don't forget that sometimes God sends angels disguised as humans to help his people.*
> *May God be with you on your journey until you find the place you are seeking."*

Then the man spoke one more time. "I have arranged for some hot food this morning and in a little while I will have the horses and your wagons brought around so that you can continue your journey."

"Thank you so much for all that you have done for us," Willy replied. "If you will give me your name and address, we will send you payment for all of this once we are settled again."

The soldier looked straight at him. "You folks don't owe me anything. Just thank the Lord that I could help you last night—and don't forget that sometimes God sends angels disguised as humans to help his people. May God be with you on your journey until you find the place you are seeking."

That night not only refreshed the group physically but also brought the assurance that they were not alone, God was still leading. As Liese settled back on the wagon next to Karli and holding tightly onto Albi she recalled God's promise. "Der Engel des HERRN lagert sich um die her, so ihn fürchten, und hilft ihnen aus." (Luther Bibel 1545) "For the angel of the Lord is a guard; he surrounds and defends all who fear him." Psalm 34:7 (NLT)

Chapter Six

Liese Finds a Resting Place

Ever mindful of the Russian Army behind them, they continued always westward. Through the refugee grapevine the group heard that the Russians had attacked the refugees some distance behind them and prevented everyone else from that point on from traveling further, diverting them back east. Willy redoubled the pace of travel and the group barely stopped except to rest and feed the horses.

One day one of the young boys, sitting at the front of the wagon, shouted: "Uncle Willy, look I think that is your brother Eric and his family!" Sure, enough, it was Eric along with two other wagons loaded with people. They all joined the caravan and traveled together. The group had now grown to more than 40 individuals. Finally, from all the road signs Willy and his brothers realized that they had arrived within the actual boundaries of Germany.

When they saw a sign with directions to the city of Wittenberg, they decided it was time to head south. As they traveled through the city they could hear the air-raid sirens screaming and the drone of the Allied bombers heading to Berlin to drop their bombs. Not knowing the destination of the bombers, they let the horses gallop as fast as they could to get out of the range of the bombers.

Once outside of the city, they stopped and looked over the map they had been able to secure earlier. The group needed a destination but none of them had ever been in Germany before and wondered where to go. As Willy studied at the map he found his attention drawn to Bavaria in southeastern Germany, particularly to the city of Neustadt an der Waldnaab, a small city by the Waldnab River near Weiden in the Oberpfalz region. That became their goal, and each day they sought out roads and highways that brought them closer. The decision to begin heading south would prove to be fortuitous.

Rather than ending up in Neustadt, the group stopped at the little farming village of Wildenreuth in northeastern Bavaria less than 25 kilometers west of the Czech border. It was late in the afternoon, and they would not have made it to their intended destination before midnight. The village was in the Bavarian Forest just off the major north-south highway called the Ostmarkstrasse (The Eastern Border Highway). Completed in 1938, Germany had built it to facilitate the movement of troops and equipment and to defend the eastern border from a Czechoslovakian invasion. Other than having both its young and middle-aged men drafted into the German armed forces, the village had not experienced fighting and destruction.

The "von Wilds," a feudal family from Prussia, had founded Wild-

Gruß aus Wildenreuth/Oberpfalz

enreuth ("Wild Clearing") in the twelfth century in the vast Bavarian Forest. A cluster of villages with names ending in the word "reuth" (clearing) dotted the region. During the 17th century the von Wild family died out and the von Podewils took over. Now the nobles no longer rule as feudal lords. The farmers are independent landowners, but the von Podewils are still very influential and their land holdings in the area are still the largest.

The village, typical of Bavarian agricultural communities, is a tight cluster of farm homes and barns surrounding the Schloss (the Baronial Manor). Farmer's fields bound the village in a big circle with the dark evergreen forest beyond. The village has one church, the St. Jakobus Simultaner Kirche (St James Simultaneous Church) used by both the Catholics and Lutherans. It also has several small businesses and general stores as well as a "gasthaus" (a German-style inn with a bar and restaurant). When the refugees arrived at the village it was considered advanced in that every dwelling had electricity and cold, running water.

The German-Bavarian dialect that the villagers spoke was initially very hard for any of the group to understand. But despite the language difficulty the people were warm and friendly. No one else fleeing the Soviet Army had yet reached the village, so it welcomed the refugees with open arms.

With most of the village men gone, and the spring farm work and planting needing to be done, the farmers were happy for the labor pool the strangers represented. The group included four adult men experienced in farm work and teenagers who could help. The Buergermeister (mayor) suggested to Willy that his group stay in Wildenreuth until the hostilities ceased. The Amis (German slang for Yanks) were advancing rapidly and would soon be in northeastern Bavaria and in Czechoslovakia. When that happened, Liese and the others could continue to wherever they needed to go. The villagers found lodging for all the families, assigning Liese and her boys to live with Christine Bergler, a single, young woman living alone in her ancestral home; she had ample room. The house was on the west end of the village, less than a kilometer east of the Ostmarkstrasse.

The trek from Lask, Poland to Wildenreuth had taken a little over two months. Liese had worried and prayed for Eddie every day. The fighting on the eastern front was furious, and nothing seemed able to halt the Russian advance. She hadn't expected to hear from him while traveling, especially as she had no permanent address and didn't know Eddie's. The daily dangers and tensions, the care for Karli and Albi, had left little time for thought and reflection.

Now that Liese was in a more permanent place she had time to think about what she and the other refugees had been through. All those days God had watched over them, providing food for them and feed for the horses. Although there had been close calls, they had kept ahead of the Red Army and everyone was safe. God had answered Eddie's parting prayer for the safety of his family.

No longer having to travel and worry about her boys' safety every day, Liese could now turn her concern to Eddie. She wondered what was he going through? Would he survive? How would she find him? How could he find her? What would happen to her and her boys? In her calmer moments Liese realized that the problems confronting her were much larger than she could solve by herself, and she asked God to give her peace of mind—and He did. Her problems and worries did not disappear, but she could focus on the tasks and opportunities at hand. Her prayers for Eddie continued, and she taught the boys to pray for their dad. Slowly the constant worry faded away.

Not long after the group arrived in Wildenreuth, the first American military vehicles began to rumble along the Ostmarkstrasse. The village leaders lost no time going to the highway with white sheets, signaling their surrender. The convoy continued on to the next city, one closer to a huge German military base called Grafenwoehr that the Americans needed to secure. For hours, the stream of trucks and tanks and jeeps roared past the village. Finally, an armored vehicle left the convoy, swung onto the road leading into the village, and stopped at the first house.

The village had signaled surrender but that might be a trap. Carefully checking the surroundings, a heavily armed soldier left the vehicle, marched up to the door, and started pounding. Fearfully, Christine Bergler, with Liese carrying Albi, opened the door. What they saw was not reassuring. The American soldier was an imposing sight. Quite tall, his machine gun was pointed straight at them! He had addressed them in German, but they couldn't get their thoughts together to answer him.

Karli maneuvered his way around his mom and faced the soldier. He knew what to do. In Kindergarten he had been taught that when confronted by a soldier you stood stiffly, clicked your heels together, raised your right arm, and shouted "Sieg Heil" (Hail the Victory). So, that is what he did. The soldier momentarily tensed, then realized that with two frightened women and a little 4-year old, the situation was not dangerous. Pushing back his helmet he said "noch einmal" (do it again). After receiving another salute, the smiling soldier fumbled through his many pockets and found what he was looking for. He rewarded Karli with a package of gum.

Karli had heard of "Kaugummi" (chewing gum) but had never had any. Now he had a whole package of it. From then on he was convinced that American soldiers were the greatest! With the more relaxed atmosphere, the women found their voices and the soldier got the information he needed, took his leave, and checked out the rest of the village. Soon American soldiers occupied the village and the war was over for Wildenreuth.

A month later, on May, 8 1945, German representatives signed the surrender documents. During the last weeks of the war, western front German officers and soldiers, recognizing the futility of further fighting, surrendered in droves, determined not to let the Russians capture them. The flood of POWs overwhelmed all Allied facilities and orderly processes. German soldiers turned in their weapons and were herded into large fenced compounds. A small force of American MPs supervised and fed them once a day. Fortunately, warm weather arrived and conditions, while tough, were bearable. As the surrender became official, the Red Cross became involved in the repatriation of POWs.

One early summer day a tall, emaciated, young German soldier in a faded and worn uniform knocked on the door. As Liese opened the door, she saw him swaying, trying desperately not to collapse. Suddenly she realized that he was her nephew, Rudolph Varesko, and he recognized her. Quickly she led him to the bed so he could rest. Then she dispatched Karli to tell his mother and sister that Rudy had come home. Running as fast as he could, the child quickly covered the short distance, raced up the stairs, and banged on the door. By then he was so out of breath, that when the door opened he could only gasp out "Rudy." It didn't take long for them all to rush quickly to Liese's and welcome Rudy home. The Americans had captured and then released him shortly afterward. The effort to locate his mother and sister had used up the last of his strength and it took him a while to recover.

A few weeks later another of the nephews, Paul Hann, came through Wildenreuth searching for his parents. He was not as fortunate as Rudy in that besides being emaciated from the privations of the war, he had been wounded and lost one of his legs. Later, a third nephew, Hans Kampen, came safely back. The British captured his two brothers, Albert and Willy, and turned them over to the Russians as they had been born in Ukraine. The Soviets sent them to a Gulag in Siberia.

On the eastern front, desperate fighting against the Russians continued until the surrender. Repatriation did not go so well there. Being MIA didn't mean that soldiers were missing in the sense that they fell off a truck or just walked off the field of battle. They were casualties for which no body had been recovered. The western Allies released their prisoners as quickly as possible, and by 1948 all but those charged with war crimes were. German soldiers who had fought on the Eastern Front and had become POWs in the U.S.S.R. remained interned for several more years. The Communists declared that since Russia had suffered such extensive damage because of the German invasion, they regarded all German POWs as an expendable labor force to use in the rebuilding the Soviet Union. They served as laborers in copper or coal mines, and anywhere between 400,000 and one million eventually died while in Russian custody. Some 20,000 former soldiers were still in Soviet hands at the time of Stalin's death in 1953, and the last 10,000 didn't get their freedom until 1955 and 1956—a full decade after the war had ended. Soviet-born ethnic Germans who had served in the German Army were released from their slave labor gulags after their 10-year sentences but could not leave the USSR.

When three of her nephews had come home after the war Liese's faith in her husband's return burned brightly for a time. But as much as she prayed and hoped for his safe return it was not to be. After many months of anxious waiting she finally received an official letter from the new provisional government of Germany stating that Eduard Konrad was "Missing in Action and Presumed Dead."

Journey from Khortitza, Ukraine to Wildenreuth, Germany
October 1943–April 1945
(Please see Explanatory Map Notes on page 103.)

Chapter Seven
Life in Wildenreuth

Liese, Karl and Albert in 1951.

Settling into the life of the village of Wildenreuth, even if it were to be only a way station, became a delightful experience. Liese, her brothers, sisters and their families all needed a breather. They had been on the move for more than 18 months since being evacuated from Khortitza and it felt good to not to hear the bombs and feel the pressures of war. The little group was not unique as more than 12 million refugees entered Germany in the weeks and months after the war ended. They arrived in a country that was in tatters and hardly had any food.

The refugees came, because they had nowhere else to go. The victors ceded the former eastern parts of Germany such as East Prussia to Poland and it expelled the Germans who had lived there. The Soviet Union did not expel its large ethnic German minorities from any of their Republics for most had dwelt there for more than 150 years. Rather they resettled them in the far eastern and northern Republics such as Kazakhstan, Kyrgyzstan, Tajikistan, Uzbekistan and Siberia.

The villagers of Wildenreuth were glad to have willing hands to help with the farm work, and the refugees were thrilled with the opportunity to work. Liese realized that her situation as a single parent with little children was not unique. She was one of many thousands of mothers whose husbands had either perished in battle or had not yet returned. All of them had the common problem of finding a way to provide the daily necessities for themselves and their children. Eventually, Liese received a small pension and a food ration card for herself and for the boys, because Eddie had served in the German Army and had been MIA. It met their basic needs. The authorities also permitted her to augment the assistance through whatever means she could find. Local agriculture was not highly mechanized and involved much manual labor. The village farmers shared the use of a potato digger, but did the grading, sorting and sacking by hand. Liese could keep the boys with her, even having them "help" her, while doing such tasks. With money in short supply, the farmers bartered potatoes and other foodstuffs for help with the harvest.

The first three to four years after war's end were extremely difficult. The cities were in ruins, winters were frigidly cold, and food and fuel were in extremely short supply. The Adventist group realized again God's guidance in leading them to Wildenreuth. The United States organized a vast relief effort. Twenty-two American aid and religious groups formed the CARE (Cooperative for American Remittances to Europe) organization. The first packages contained surplus military field rations. Eventually running out of them, CARE made up packages that contained staples, rice, beans, powdered eggs, powdered milk, shortening, flour, sugar, and coffee.

When the packages first arrived in Wildenreuth labeled "CARE Gift Package," the word "Gift" panicked people because in German the word for "poison" is "gift." Finally, someone with a rudimentary knowledge of English told them that the word "gift" was the English equivalent for the German "Geschenk" ("present"). With much relief, everyone gratefully accepted and used the packages. Later, Adventist Church members in America obtained names and addresses of Adventists in Germany and sent packages with the help of the CARE organization.

Liese received some of the packages and made good use of the contents. Items she could not use she exchanged with others who could. She was enough of a seamstress so that the used clothes she received she cleaned, altered, and pressed until they looked and fit as if made to order. One of the Adventist parcels contained a jar of peanut butter. She recognized that it was a spread made from "Errdnuesse" ("peanuts"). The idea of PB and J sandwiches was not part of her taste horizon. But if you took a freshly boiled potato, sliced it, and spread it with peanut butter, it made the potato slice special and the jar was soon empty.

While Liese enjoyed living with Kristine Bergler, because they got along well, eventually she had to find a new place to live. Kristine was appointed to serve as the new post mistress for the village. The post office would be located at her house, taking up the room Liese and the boys lived in. She obtained an upstairs room near the center of the village. Her new landlady was also a single mother with several children. But when the woman's husband finally came home from the war, Liese and boys had to move once more. She soon found a good sized upstairs room in a farmhouse where she was not the only renter, and that is where she lived for the rest of her stay in Wildenreuth.

In late fall with the harvest over and the weather colder, one of the farm women complained to Liese that she needed some warm house shoes but had not been able to locate any for sale or barter. Farmers usually wore wooden clogs while doing chores and then changed to slippers or house shoes when finished with the barn work. "Do you have any heavy winter coats that you are no longer using?" Liese asked. "If you will let me have them, I am sure that I can make you a beautiful pair house shoes."

Quickly answering, "I sure do!" she ran to get the old unused coats. Liese traced an outline of her feet on old butcher's paper that the woman had. When she got home she cut the material for the soles, and glued several layers together with wheat starch paste. Liese's brother Willy lent her some wooden lasts, which she used to shape the upper part of the shoe. After sewing a design into the uppers, she stitched them to the soles. Using an awl to punch through soles, she used strong, beeswaxed thread and a stout needle to do the sewing. Mr. Haus, an experienced blacksmith and fellow refugee, made the needle from a discarded umbrella rib. The Bauernfrau (farmwife) was so delighted with the house shoes that she had to show them off to all her women friends. Soon Liese had a backlog of orders and realized that God was answering several of her prayers.

Making house shoes was something she could do at home while watching the boys, it contributed to the upkeep of the family, and gave her a natural way to have contact with the villagers. While taking foot measurements and discussing designs and colors, the conversation with the women would often turn to spiritual topics. They noticed that while her husband had not returned from the fighting, Liese maintained a calm outlook. Instead of flirting with the American soldiers or any of the other men, she worked hard to be productive and raise her boys. Liese told them how God had protected her and her family on their trek, guided them to Wildenreuth, and calmed her anxious thoughts about Eddie, and now the Lord was helping her deal with the rising panic of being a single parent. Having opportunity to share her testimony of God's goodness was very important to her. Remembering the promise that she had made years ago at her baptism that she would be an active Christian witness, she felt at a loss as to how she could do that in Wildenreuth. She prayed that God would open a way for her to live out her commitment.

Another woman, who heard all the good reports about Liese, finally got up her courage to go see her. Extremely self-conscious about her misshapen foot, she had a terrible time finding comfortable footwear. Approaching Liese, she asked, "Is there a way that you could make a special slipper to fit my foot?" Unsure just how to accomplish that difficult task, Liese examined the foot thoroughly, but the woman's tone revealed how much she needed encouragement and help. With a quick, silent prayer Liese asked the woman to stand on a piece of paper so that she could make a proper outline. As she was drawing carefully, a plan formulated in her mind, and she told the woman, "I will make you a pair of house slippers that not only will fit your foot but will also look beautiful and stylish."

In a much happier tone the woman showed Liese the material she had brought and described the designs she wanted. They agreed on a completion date and the woman left in a cheerful frame of mind. Liese realized that God was guiding her in the work. When the woman came to pick up her shoes, she was amazed at how good they looked and how well they fit. She was ecstatic.

One day a younger woman knocked on the door and introduced herself. "My name is Bertha Lehnert, I am the daughter of the retired, Lutheran village schoolmaster and would like you to make a pair of house shoes for my mother." After discussing how she wanted the house shoes to look, she shared some things about herself. Bertha had completed the rigorous teacher training course and had not been teaching long. Recently returned to Wildenreuth to make sure her parents were doing well, she had noticed that much had changed in the village during her absence and with the ending of the war. The Adventist refugees now living in the village especially intrigued her. Liese shared with her how God had led the group to Wildenreuth and the principles that guided their life. The visit made Bertha even more interested, and she took the initiative to become acquainted with others in the Adventist group, becoming especially close to Hilda Varesko, Liese's niece. After time spent with Hilda, Liese and other members of the little community of believers, as well as many hours of Bible studies with Willy, she requested baptism.

Her decision precipitated a twofold crisis with her parents and with her position as a teacher. She had been open with her parents about her spiritual journey and what she was planning to do with what she was learning. They could not comprehend her position. As far as they were concerned, she was throwing away her future. But knowing the careful thought that had gone in to making her decision they did not openly oppose it. On the other hand, the school board reminded her that the German Educational system ran six days a week, Monday through Saturday, with no exceptions. If she could not or would not meet that schedule, she would have to resign. And without further discussion Bertha did exactly that.

Facing an uncertain future, Bertha prayed for God's guidance. Her prayer led her to attend the Adventist Church's recently re-opened Seminar Marienhoehe in Darmstadt to take the Bible Workers course of study. After her actual arrival at the school the administrators there discovered her advanced academic teaching credentials and asked her to join the faculty and teach in upper elementary grades as well as some of the beginning ministerial courses. While at the school she met a young man, eventually they married, and together they worked for the church in various capacities through the years.

In the summer of 1952, a couple of months after Liese and boys had arrived and settled in America, they received a letter from Bertha. "Dear Liese," she wrote, "how empty Wildenreuth seems to me with all of your family gone to America. All the villagers miss having you folks around and have nothing but good

We are now separated by distance but joined together in the same faith. You were the very first person that shared these wonderful truths with me.

memories of your stay here. Whenever I visit my mom in Wildenreuth we quietly celebrate God's Sabbath together in her garden. How wonderful God was in introducing us to each other. We are now separated by distance but joined together in the same faith. You were the very first person that shared these wonderful truths with me. Thank you for doing that. In Christian Love, Bertha." The letter was an inspiration to Liese, and she kept it as a reminder of God's answer to her prayer about being a witness of His truth. All the hard work of measuring, cutting, gluing, and stitching had led to the salvation of one person to Christ, and Liese felt well repaid.

Liese was not alone among the group in finding work that would help provide income for the families. Her sisters and other women of the refugee group could earn cash or barter for food or clothing by cleaning the houses of the wealthier villagers. Each of her brothers soon found work that suited their skills and experience. Gerhard used his horses to transport people and things from place to place. Willy opened a shoe repair shop. So much work flooded it that he could employ two of his nephews who had come back from the war. The cobbler shop eventually consisted of five men from the refugee group repairing and making new shoes from leather obtained from the nearby city of Erbendorf.

Willy organized all the relatives and friends who ended up in and near Wildenreuth into a church group that met every Sabbath. The group asked him to serve as the pastor of the little company and requested Brother Haus to be the Head Elder. Liese's sister, Else, taught the children's Sabbath school. They had held those positions in the church at Khortitza and wherever the group had lived during the long trek out of Russia. They worshipped and witnessed to their faith without any initial contact with other like-minded believers in the region. The locals told them that Hitler had imprisoned and killed all the Seventh-day Adventists in the area. But that was not the case. Adventist believers were living in nearby cities, and word soon reached the local conference office in Nuremberg that the village of Wildenreuth had a group of Sabbath-observing refugees.

Uncle Willy's Congregation in Wildenreuth (1947)

Before long the conference president came to talk to Willy. The visit resulted in Willy becoming the full-time pastor of the small group as well as two other churches in the region. The Wildenreuth group had 28 adult members with at least another dozen or so children. The other two churches in Weiden and Marktredwitz included another 95 adult members. The conference provided a bicycle for Willy to use in his ministry to the three congregations. The General Conference had paid for the bicycles as money and automobiles were not readily available in Germany right after the war. When conditions improved, Willy graduated to a light motorcycle.

Sabbaths for the little group in Wildenreuth meant Sabbath School and Church in the mornings and then lunch at home. When Willy spoke at one of his other churches, his brother Gerhard or the head elder took the responsibility of preaching. Most of the spring, summer and autumn Sabbath afternoons were spent hiking in the Bavarian Forest surrounding the village. Often everyone brought their various musical instruments to play at the midpoint of the hike. Then the group would rest and celebrate the Sabbath and leave in time to get back before dark.

Even though times were difficult Liese realized that birthdays and holidays needed something extra. She did her best to surprise the boys on these occasions. One Christmas she traded tobacco ration cards and some coffee that came in one of the CARE packages for Italian oranges as well as two red wind-up toy VW cars. Along with the customary hazel nuts, walnuts, and cookies, it made for a memorable Christmas.

When conditions eased, she had a tailor make the traditional Bavarian dress jacket for the boys. Fashioned from heavy, gray woolen cloth, they had green oak leaf trim, red piping, and deer antler buttons. For his fourth grade, she got Karl a pair of "Lederhosen" (leather shorts). That year their winter shoes were ski boots, and for Christmas Liese had a local woodworker make a sturdy sled with iron shod runners and a pair of skis for Karl. The boys spent a lot of time outside that winter.

Sabbath afternoon in the woods and Karl is playing the violin (1951).

Their days in Wildenreuth became weeks then months, and finally years. The seasons made their appointed rounds, and one fall after the 1947 harvest was complete it was time for Karl to begin school. That year all the village students attended the same school. Since religious instruction was part of the public school curriculum, the villagers wondered how to accomplish that part of the schooling since both Catholic and Lutheran students attended the same school.

By the next year the village had two schools, one for the Lutherans and the other for the Catholics. The Adventist refugees were determined to be Protestants and their children attended the Lutheran school. However they had friends on both sides of the "divide." Albert started first grade in the fall of 1949.

Liese, like the other parents in the Adventist group, made arrangements for the boys not to attend school on Saturdays. On Fridays, the teachers would give them a "heads up" about what would be taught the next day. It was boy's responsibility to get the work done without the help of the teacher's directions. Liese saw that Karl favored his left hand in many activities. Had he grown up in America he would have been encouraged to grow up a "lefty." But in Germany the educational system taught everyone to write with their right hand, no exceptions. Karl did learn to write right handed, but his penmanship left something to be desired. His teacher always noted in his report cards that his handwriting needed much improvement.

Chapter Eight
Boys Will Be Boys

Both Karl and Albert easily made friends with the village boys. Albert found as his best friend, Wilfried, who was the same age and in the same grade. The boy's father was also one of the MIAs from the eastern front and like Albert's dad never did return from the fighting. Karl had several good friends; his two best buddies were Hermann Schieder, son of a local farm family, and Reinhardt Schmidt, whose father was the town's Lutheran Pastor. Being a couple of years older than Albert, Karl was more active and busy doing "the growing-up" things boys do.

One day as Karl and Hermann were playing, a returning solder stopped to observe them, glancing from one boy to the other. They both had blond hair and blue

Karl, Albert and a friendly dog in 1948.

eyes and were quite skinny. After gazing steadily at Karl's friend, Hermann, he recognized who he was and called out his name, "Hermann, Hermann, my son!" Immediately the lad dropped everything and ran into his father's outstretched arms. What a wonderful day it turned out to be for the Schieder family. Karl watched the reunion of his friend with his father and wondered if his dad would one day show up, call his name and wrap his arms around him like that.

Karl and Hermann always seemed to be spending time together keeping busy helping with farm chores. One day they were riding in the back of the Schieder's cow-drawn wagon down a narrow lane to the farm's root cellar to load mangels (a beet-like root vegetable that was used as livestock fodder). During the loading, the boys balanced on the wagon's sideboards. A fly bit one of the cows and she jerked the wagon forward. Losing his balance, Karl fell out of the wagon and wedged between the wagon wheel and some posts laying at the edge of the lane. As the wheel moved the rusty iron rim scraped down the side of his cheek and abraded the skin.

When Hermann looked down all he could see was Karl's bloody head and body lying seemingly lifeless on the ground. He began to yell as loudly as he could, "Er is tot! Er is tot!" ("He is dead! He is dead!"). By the time Hermann's parents made their way to the far side of the wagon Karl was coming to, but his face continued to bleed profusely. They examined him and saw that he could move his arms, that his jaw was working, despite his tears he could still speak, and the flow of blood slowed to a trickle. Quickly they took him home so that his mother could treat the injury.

Hermann's parents discovered that the local area doctor was at the Baronial manor for a medical visit with the Baroness, so they contacted him. When told of Karl's injury, the physician agreed to stop by and check it out. He concluded that Karl had probably experienced a concussion but that his injuries were only surface wounds and would heal. Liese had cleaned them well, and the only problem that he could foresee was the possible infection that might result from the contaminated materials that had been ground into Karl's cheek. He promised to stop by in a couple of weeks when he came to do a follow-up visit for the Baroness.

The skin abrasions healed quickly but an infection did set in underneath the healed skin. Soon Karl sported a large protrusion on the left side of his face. Worried, Liese wondered what she could do to treat the infection. Then she remembered that in her youth her mom had used a flax-seed poultice to heal a boil. The poultice would soften the skin to the point that the boil would burst open and release the pus. She obtained some flax seed from one of the local farmers and boiled it into a mucilage (a gelatinous liquid substance). With it she made a poultice and placed it over the boil. Repeating it for several more days, she saw that the skin was getting softer and softer and was sure that in just a couple more days the boil would burst of its own accord.

But the boil had remained intact. There was a knock on the door and a cheery "Guten Tag Frau Konrad" as the doctor peeked in. "I realize I am a few days early, but I received a call to check on the Baroness today. I have done that and thought that since I am in the area I would check in on my young patient." When Karl stood before him, the good doctor saw his lopsided face and exclaimed, "What have we here!" Liese undid the poultice that had covered the wound so that he could have a closer look. Examining the swelling and feeling the softness of the skin, he told Liese, "You know that poultice of yours was exactly the right thing to do. It is ready for lancing, so Frau Konrad, eine Schuessel bitte!" ("Mrs. Konrad please bring a large bowl.") Quickly she found one and lifted it to the left side of Karl's face. The doctor carefully wiped his lance and made a swift thrust into the cheek. As the discharge filled the bowl he gently massaged the cheek to get the last of the fluid out of the wound and then disinfected and bandaged the incision.

Albert had been sitting quietly on the other side of the room where he could watch the whole procedure. As the doctor pulled out the knife to lance the boil, Albert's eyes kept getting bigger and bigger. When he saw the doctor start to plunge the knife into Karl's face, it was more than he could take. Unable to be quiet any longer, he jumped up out of his seat, charged toward the doctor, and yelled, "Don't you dare hurt my brother!" The physician simply put his arm around Albert and said, "Look, young man, doesn't his cheek look better now. That big bad old boil is all gone!" Sure, enough, Karl did indeed look semi-normal. Satisfied that his brother was not hurt, Albert apologized. The cheek did heal with only a tiny scar as a reminder of the incident.

Both boys tried their best to behave and be obedient while their mother made slippers or delivered them. But at times their best intention gave way to the mischievousness of growing boys.

Both boys tried their best to behave and be obedient while their mother made slippers or delivered them. But at times their best intention gave way to the mischievousness of growing boys. They never set out to get into to trouble, sometimes it just seemed to come upon them unawares. One Friday afternoon the boys were all cleaned up and ready for the Sabbath and for that evening's youth meeting at Uncle Willy's place. Liese had boiled a pot full of potatoes that would part of that evening's meal as well as the basis for a potato salad for the next day. She asked the boys to stay in the apartment and behave as she quickly went out to deliver a pair of slippers that she had made for one of the village women. Both of her sons promised that they would be good and not fight with each other.

Liese hadn't been gone for more than just a few minutes before they heard Karl's name being called up from the street below. His friends intended to fight with several other boys, and they needed Karl to help them get the upper hand. Karl always did his best to be obedient and shouted back to them, "I can't come. I promised my mom to watch my little brother, and I can't leave him alone."

"But we need your help," they shouted. "Some guys are chasing us and are about to catch us. Can't you see them! They are going clobber us unless you help us. You got to do something!" Glancing around, Karl saw the pot of potatoes cooling on the stove.

Karli and Albi (1947).

"I got an idea," he yelled back. "I will lob out some potatoes that you can use to throw at them. OK?"

"That's better than nothing" they replied. So, Karl chose a couple of potatoes and gently tossed them to his friends. But two were not enough and before he realized he and Albert had emptied most of the potatoes from the pot. But Karl's friends had fended off the "enemies," and they thanked him for his help.

Now reality settled in for Karl as he looked at the mostly empty pot. Turning to Albert, he said, "When mom comes, you just keep quiet and let me do all the talking. You hear!"

"OK, Karl. I will." With that both boys got out their books, settled down and practiced looking innocent. Liese knew what had happened before she even opened the door. She had seen peelings and pieces of cooked potatoes all over the street just outside of the front door of the house. Though both boys tried their best to play innocent, the truth quickly came out between their cries as their mother meted out punishment.

Dusk comes early during Bavarian winters. Evenings are long. Albert had come straight home from school, but Karl had not yet arrived. He was, after all, a third grader and more on his own. As time passed and he did not appear, Liese began to worry. She and Albert were about to put on their coats to go and look for him when she heard someone coming up the stairs. Hearing a knock on the door, she hurriedly opened it and was speechless at the sight that met her eyes.

Paul Metzger, one of the men from the village, stood there with Karl in tow. The boy was dripping wet from the top of his head to the bottom of his feet. Icicles were hanging off his coat sleeves. As he shivered violently, his skin color was white as the snow and his teeth were chattering so much that he could not speak.

Before Liese could ask what happened, Herr Metzger began to explain. "Frau Konrad, I thought I was home for the evening but I suddenly remembered that I had an appointment with the Mayor and headed toward his house to keep it. On my way, I was walking past the pond when I heard a voice yelling 'Hilfe, Hilfe, bitte Hilfe!' ("Help, Help, please Help!") I looked in the direction from where the cries came and saw a head bobbing up and down in the broken ice. I followed his footprints and slide marks to get close to where the head was. When I got near I laid down on the ice and crawled closer still. Then I told him to work his way toward me until I was finally able to get hold of his arm and pull him out. You will have to ask him why he was on the ice. I don't know why he was on it, especially since we harvested it just yesterday. It did freeze some overnight but it was not thick enough to support anyone."

All Liese could say was, "Herr Metzger, I am so glad that you heard his cries and rescued him. Thank you! Thank you! We will always be in debt to you for saving him." "God is good and all is well," he responded. "And now I must be on my way."

Quickly Liese heated water on the stove and helped Karl get out of his wet and frozen clothes. After wrapping him in the grey, woolen Wehrmacht (army) blanket that Eddie had left with them in Poland, she made him some hot peppermint tea. With the bath warming him from the outside and the tea from the inside, the shivering eventually stopped. "Karl, why were you on the ice?" she now asked him.

"Well," he stammered, "I was on my way home and passed the pond. There was just a thin layer of snow covering the ice and it looked so smooth and inviting. I just wanted to see how far I could slide after a good run. Mama, I got up to a good speed and slid a long way. After that first slide, I just had to do another. I had forgotten about the ice harvesting yesterday. I was on my last slide when I reached the thin ice and broke through. The water was so cold and I was so scared that I didn't even think to pray. I tried to crawl back up on the ice but kept breaking through. The harder

I tried, the more I headed toward the thinner ice. That is when I started screaming for help. When Herr Metzger came out on the ice he stayed back where I first broke through and told me to work my way back him. When I was close enough he was able to grab me, and pull me out."

"Karl Konrad! You sure have frightened me! And you almost drowned. If it had not been for our good neighbor, you would have died today. This is not the first time you have gotten into trouble by not obeying and thinking things through. I am worried about your carelessness. You know that it was your guardian angel that prompted Herr Metzger to remember his appointment to see the mayor and to go right then? You need to be much more careful about what you get yourself into. Come, let's have our good night prayer and thank Jesus for once again saving your life." With grateful hearts, they all prayed. Karl and Albert quickly fell asleep, leaving their mother alone and awake to worry about the future of her boys.

Karl and Albert ready for
America (1951).

Chapter Nine
Coming to America

The Nazi government had declared Liese and her sons German citizens in 1944, and the new West German government validated their citizenship in 1949, issuing a new passport. But she realized, however, that as a single parent the opportunities for her and the boys were limited. She recalled some of her and Eddie's early marriage dreams. They had decided that if they ever had the opportunity to leave Communist rule, they would do their best to go to America. Eddie's uncle Eduard Remfert had immigrated to Canada in 1928. And in 1948 she heard that another of Eddie's uncles, Theodore Remfert and his family, were leaving Germany to go to Canada. The news spurred her and her brothers and sisters to seek immigration for themselves. Liese began the application process that turned out to be long and arduous. It involved endless forms to be completed and medical exams to undergo.

Liese, the boys and all her relatives who chose to come to America did so because of the Displaced Persons Act (DPA) signed by American President Harry S. Truman on June 16, 1950, allowing entry for 200,000 refugees, including acceptance of 55,000 ethnic Germans displaced from their original place of residence due to the war. It was the second DPA that President Truman had authorized. The first, signed on June 25, 1948, allowed entry for 200,000 European refugees, but did not include displaced people from Russia or other Eastern European countries. Eventually a third DPA under President Dwight Eisenhower in 1953 permitted another 200,000 to come to the United States.

The United Nations International Refugee Organization (IRO), a temporary specialized agency of the United Nations, oversaw the humanitarian effort. Between its formal establishment in 1946 and its termination in January 1952, it assisted refugees and displaced persons in many countries of Europe and Asia who either could not return to their countries of origin or were unwilling for political reasons. Beginning operation on July 1, 1947, the IRO took over the work of its principal predecessor organization, the United Nations Relief and Rehabilitation Administration. Among the services the IRO offered were the care and maintenance of refugees in camps, vocational training, orientation for resettlement, and an extensive tracking service to find lost relatives. It also assumed the responsibilities for the legal protection and resettlement of refugees.

For Liese and her family the legal sponsoring organization was the Christian World Service (CWS), the relief, development, and refugee assistance arm of the National Council of the Churches of Christ, an ecumenical consortium of Christian denominations in America. The various groups worked with CWS to find sponsors for refugees from their own denomination. Each immigrant and all of their family members needed a sponsor in the United States who would guarantee a place to live and work for the first year. Each sponsor was also responsible for transportation costs from the port of entry to their destination. The immigrants were to reimburse their sponsor for this cost during their first year. Within two and a half months after arriving in America Liese was able to repay her sponsor the full $81.00 expense he incurred. The General Conference of Seventh-day Adventists in conjunction with the CWS arranged the sponsorships for all of Liese's relatives.

Gerhard and Liese's families traveling to Bremen Haven bound for America (1952).

The preparations for the immigration to America took longer than expected. The initial plan called for Liese and her sons to come to America in 1951, and travel with her brother Willy. They spent some time in a Displaced Persons Pre-Immigration Site located in Munich.

There they received medical exams and once again their paperwork was checked in preparation for the trip to America. Because of some delay in the paper work, Liese and both boys were rescheduled to leave in February, 1952 at same time that her brother, Gerhard, and his family would leave.

In January the two families received orders to proceed to Bremer-Haven in northern Germany for final processing. This time everything was in order, and they received clearance to travel to America. Liese, the boys, and Gerhard, his wife and three daughters boarded the ship, the *General C.H. Muir*, docked in Bremerhaven. The

Though America provided opportunity and education it did bring to permanent reality the separation that had begun back in October of 1943 as they fled Ukraine.

ship left harbor on Saturday, February 23, 1952 and docked in New York Harbor on Tuesday, March 4, 1952.

The ship had been a troop carrier for the United States Navy during the later stages of WW2 and after the war. During the 1950's the ship served as transport for displaced refugees from Europe. It is interesting to note that the journey out of Lask, Poland also began on a Saturday, but both journeys ended in safety and freedom. War and its aftermath were never a respecter of the seventh-day Sabbath or the prayer of Jesus in Matthew 24:20: "Pray that your flight will not take place in winter or on the Sabbath." (NIV)

Liese's brothers and sisters had lived near each other both in Ukraine and in Germany but when they came to America they found themselves scattered all over the country from Kansas to Michigan as well as Oregon. Though America provided opportunity and education it did bring to permanent reality the separation that had begun back in October of 1943 as they fled Ukraine. Though the Hann family had reunions from time to time, they never moved to be in the close proximity they had in Ukraine.

During the 10-day trip across the northern Atlantic Ocean the ship encountered severe winter weather. While her boys and her brother's family were sea sick for most of the crossing, Liese was in robust health for the entire trip. The fresh sea air and her hope of a new life energized her. She would be eating an apple and at the same time be holding a bag for the boys or some other family member to fill it with the contents of their stomach.

The vessel had no facilities to house families together. The men were bunked near the middle of the ship, the women toward the front, with cabins reserved for the aged and for mothers with very small children. Mothers with small children as well as the elderly received seats in the former officer's dining room, but the rest ate their meals at standing height tables. The ship's officers assigned women to help in the kitchen and the men would clean the deck or the engine room.

As the ship drew closer to harbor in New York City, the Captain and crew threw a party for all the children. They showed cartoons of Mickey Mouse, Woody Woodpecker, Goofy, Tom and Jerry as well as Donald Duck. The party culminated in the children receiving all the cake and Neapolitan ice cream that they could eat. Karl and Albert had tasted ice cream before, but never three flavors at one time. What a wonderful place America was going to be, they thought, when you get ice cream for no special reason and you could eat all that you wanted.

Letzter Gruß aus Bremen vor der Überfahrt   MS. „GENERAL C. H. MUIR"

The ship that brought Liese and the boys safely to America.

America no longer processed immigrants through Ellis Island. It now served other purposes, first as a detention and deportation center for illegal immigrants, then during World War 2 as a hospital for wounded soldiers, and later as a Coast Guard training center until permanently closed in 1954.

When the ship finally docked they disembarked, were guided to a large hall, and formed into long lines. Standing by their shipboard luggage they waited for the customs inspector to go through their belongings. Here a representative from the General Conference of Seventh-day Adventists (GC) met the Adventist immigrants. The GC had made arrangements with US Customs and assured them that the Adventist luggage would contain no contraband materials (tobacco, liquor, and firearms). When the inspector arrived, he just stickered the luggage and cleared them to leave.

GC reps then guided the Adventist immigrants to their respective railroad stations. Liese and the boys were scheduled to board a Grand Trunk Western RR train that would take them to Holly, Michigan. Gerhard and family, at a different station, were traveling by train all the way west to Eugene, Oregon. The GC reps provided enough money to purchase food for the trip and saw to it they were at the correct gates to board their particular trains.

Liese's sponsor was a Seventh-day Adventist minister by the name of Elder Ulrich Bender who lived in the small town of Holly. Its population was about 3,000 people and was mostly a bedroom community for the men that worked in the auto plants located in either Flint, Pontiac or Detroit. Elder Bender had started in the Adventist ministry in 1898. He and his wife were both 74 years old, had two grown children, were retired and later moved to Florida.

Elder Bender had written a letter to Liese dated November 4, 1951 as a way of introducing himself as her sponsor and giving her encouragement to undertake the journey. He mentioned the opportunities her sons would have. "In America your two boys can learn anything they want to learn. It will require time and patience and work. May the Lord bless you and direct your path to us, if that is His will. Your friend, U. Bender."

Liese determined that she would do all in her power to make sure that Karl and Albert would be able to learn all that was needed to be successful in America. She wanted much more than what had been afforded to her in Russia as a child. Even in Germany, with its excellent education system, preparation for a university education began with fifth grade, and as a single parent she did not have the resources to have Karl attend the Gymnasium (a specialized school in Germany, Scandinavia, and central Europe that prepares pupils for university entrance) in Weiden when he started fifth grade. She determined that in America, with God's help, her boys would be educated and a blessing to God's church.

Chapter Ten

Life in Holly, Michigan

The train trip from New York was an over-nighter, and they arrived at the Holly station the afternoon of the next day. Liese and the boys got off the train and looked around. In March Michigan is still cold, and while a lot of the snow has already melted, one can expect still more. The trees were still bare and the landscape dreary. Elder and Mrs. Bender met them at the station. Mrs. Piekarek, the wife from the other German family they had sponsored, was with them to translate. Bender loaded the car and drove them to where they would be staying. One of the church members, Mrs. C.B. Hirlinger, an elderly widow, had volunteered to open her home for them until they could move to their own apartment.

The boys slept in the enclosed front porch. Overnight the temperature dropped below freezing and it snowed. Although they had enough blankets to keep warm, the room was cold and the snowflakes that drifted through the cracks onto the bed did not melt. A hot breakfast got them going early. Having both bananas and oranges at the same time was special. Mrs. Hirlinger made a lunch for the boys, and they were ready to go. School in America began for them that morning!

They would attend the local church school sponsored by the Holly Seventh-day Adventist Church. Church members had made arrangements to pay the tuition charges. Their American education would not end until both Karl and Albert achieved all their educational goals. Along the way God provided the means, the will, and the energy necessary.

One of the teenage boys from the neighborhood, a seventh grader, stopped by to show Karl and Albert the way to school. The short way was to cross the rail road track and cut through a meadow. The two-room school building was brand new with grades one through four in one room and grades five through eight in the other. The teachers knew that Karl had started fifth grade and Albert third grade in Germany the previous fall. The boys did not speak or read English so the school decided that for the remainder of the school year it would keep the boys together in the same room to get acclimated to American education and learn English. The teacher assigned Karl to do fourth grade classwork and Albert second-grade lessons. If they achieved English language proficiency, then next fall Karl would enter the sixth grade and Albert the fourth.

Learning English was not a problem for the boys since no one spoke German in their classroom. They picked up the language from the American kids and acquired a Michigan accent. Only their mother and the Piekareks could speak to them in their mother tongue. Of course, they conversed with their mother daily, but since everyone was always busy, get-togethers with the other German family were hard to schedule. Within weeks the boys were attempting conversations and soon were fluent enough with English to make friends and keep up with school work.

For Liese, learning English did not come quite so easy, and the first several months were difficult. It was frustrating especially when she and the boys would go to church. The Holly Adventist Church was just a couple of blocks from Mrs. Hirlinger's place, an easy walk each Sabbath. Many of

For Liese, learning English did not come quite so easy, and the first several months were difficult.

the church members, to be friendly, had learned a few German phrases such as "Wie geht's?" ("How is it going?") and usually managed them in passable German. Liese would answer with the appropriate German words only to discover that they could not understand her, the extent of their German being that two-word expression.

One Sabbath a young family man, Roland Neufeld, asked the question in excellent German and in the longer version "Wie geht es ihnen heute?" Not only was his German great, he also spoke to her in "Plattdeutsch" or

"Low-German," the dialect that Liese and her brothers and sisters spoke among themselves. It turned out that he had grown up in a Canadian-German Adventist farmer/preacher family whose forebears had originated in Ukraine. He had served in the Canadian Air Force as a radar operator during the war and been stationed in England. There he met a young British Adventist woman, named Jean, whom he had courted, married and brought to Canada.

The Neufelds had recently immigrated to the USA and were living in Holly. Roland, in partnership with another church member, Harold Lutz, was a finish carpentry subcontractor for a large real estate developer in nearby Flint. Business was booming, and they were busy. Liese and the boys became friends with both families. Recently, Albert reminisced to Karl that "they took us under their wings and made sure that we got started right." Roland and Jean had two children, Janice and Rolly (Roland, Jr.), while Harold and Evelyn had one daughter, Cherie. The children became attached to Liese, and she often babysat them. They called her "Tante Liese" (Aunt Liese). They loved the stories she told them in her broken English.

Liese realized that the living arrangements with Mrs. Hirlinger were only temporary, a bridge to help her reach independence. In addition to helping with the cooking and house cleaning at home, Liese developed a house cleaning route and began earning a regular income. Mrs. Hirlinger's house was small, and now with four persons living in it, two of them active boys, it felt rather crowded and at times noisy. With two growing youngsters, food disappeared at a prodigious rate. Years before, Mrs. Hirlinger and her husband developed, manufactured, and sold throughout the USA a vegetarian product called "Sovex," a yeast-vegetable concentrate used as a flavoring base for making gravy, soup or bouillon. It was like the popular Australian "Marmite" and "Vegemite." The Australians love those spreads on bread or crackers. But in American only a few hearty souls used "Sovex" as a spread for bread, crackers and sandwiches. Mrs. Hirlinger still owned, made, and marketed the product at the time Liese and the boys arrived in America. While she meant well and considered "Sovex" to be part of a healthy meal, it was an acquired taste that eluded the boys, especially when spread on Graham crackers as a school lunch treat.

One time when Liese was baby-sitting the Neufeld children, she told Roland that she needed a place of her own where she could provide the kind of food her boys were used to eating. It would also help if it was closer to the places where she cleaned houses and cooked for her clients. Roland told her that he had heard of a three-room apartment located near the center of Holly and would check it out for her. It was not long until with the help of the members of the church Liese not only had a place of her own but also all the necessary furniture to fill it.

Liese and her sons quickly settled into the apartment. The three rooms with a bath were located on the second floor of what used to be the former Adventist Conference president's house, right next door to the old Eastern Michigan Conference of Seventh-day Adventists headquarters building. It was also across the street from the Neufeld's apartment. Compared to the cramped living quarters they had had in Germany, it was spacious. The Lutz's let her use their camp meeting "ice-box" cabinet to keep things cool. It required a 25-pound block of ice that needed replacing at least every four or five days. Later one of the church members purchased a new refrigerator and sold the old one to Liese for $25. It was a wonderful addition since it kept things colder without them having to worry about the melting ice.

The refrigerator was old, but did its job with few exceptions. After a couple years it finally quit working. Liese told the boys that they would have to do without the fridge. "I just cannot afford to fix it, and I am afraid much of our food will spoil." Karl and Albert looked up from the Parcheesi game they were playing on the kitchen table. "Don't worry, mom," Karl said. "Maybe Mr. Lutz can fix it again. I'll ask him."

"Karl, let's not bother him." Liese sighed and said, "he has been good to us and has fixed it before, but this time I think it needs a professional repair man to check it out. We just don't have the money to do that right now."

After putting away the clothes that she had been folding, she slipped on her coat. "I have to go across the street to stay with the Neufeld children for a while. Boys, be good while I am gone and be sure to go to bed when it is time."

"We promise" both said in unison.

The game now had less interest than before as the boys tried to think about what could be done about the fridge. Albert finally broke the silence, looked at Karl and said, "I sure wish we knew how to fix it. Then mom would not have to spend money on it."

"You know it's not only getting it fixed that worries her," Karl replied, "it is also the food that will spoil if the fridge doesn't run."

"I know. Maybe there is something that we both could do. We could pray and ask Jesus to help us."

"You are right, Albert, we could and should pray. So, let's do it now. Jesus knows all about it and how much we need to have it fixed."

Karl and Albert knelt beside that old fridge and asked God to repair it. When they got up from their knees, Karl turned up the cooling dial and the motor began to hum once again. It was not just a temporary fix for it continued to run until Liese saved up enough money for the down payment of a brand new Frigidaire.

> *"I know. Maybe there is something that we both could do. We could pray and ask Jesus to help us."*

Liese's sponsor, Elder Bender, had arranged a position for her in a rest home helping to care for the elderly individuals who lived there. She would be working with Mrs. Piekarek. By the time Liese arrived the facility did not have enough residents to keep both women busy.

Bender and other members of the Holly Church contacted several of the town's wealthier families for her to clean their houses. Word soon spread of her excellent work cleaning as well as cooking and caring for their children. One of the ladies that Liese worked for wrote, "Cooking, cleaning, whatever Elizabeth did, was to perfection…not a speck of dirt was allowed in her presence. Her delicious kuchen would melt in your mouth. We came to enjoy several German dishes. I can't remember the names but my favorite was a potato mixture folded inside a light flakey crust. They were good hot or cold. One Saturday night, my husband and I were awakened by a policeman at our front door. My father had been in a terrible accident, and we had to rush to a Flint hospital. Instead of having to wake our 8-year-old daughter and take her to someone else's house, Elisabeth gladly came to our house and was there in the morning to explain everything to our daughter, Cheri, and comfort her."

No matter how hard or how much she and the boys worked they never seemed to have enough money to do many of the extra things in life. But because they were willing to do whatever was necessary to earn money, they did have all the essentials of life. She paid the rent on time, and the table always had food on it. Liese cleaned houses, churches, offices, and cooked and cared for children whenever and wherever she could. The boys raked leaves, swept sidewalks, mowed lawns with old fashioned push lawnmowers, and sold bread and rolls that Liese baked. Together they never left a job unturned.

Seldom did Liese have to discipline her sons. When they were younger she did have to spank them on one or two occasions. But when the boys became teenagers she no longer used corporal punishment. Instead she could "guilt" them into obedience. For Karl, it was the simple reminder that she had protected him time and time again during the bombing raids that occurred when he was a baby. On one occasion, she reminded him, that she had broken several ribs when in their frantic rush to safety she fell down the stairs into the shelter. For Albert, it was the story of only having three diapers when they were fleeing in the dead of winter. She had to take the one she had just washed and wrap it around herself and let her body heat dry it.

On one occasion Albert got himself into trouble by experimenting with smoking cigarettes. He thought he had covered his tracks by chewing a whole pack of gum and using several "Sen-Sen" chiclets, then brushing his teeth and running outside to get the smell off him and his clothes. But the adage "be sure your sins will find you out" once again proved its validity. Liese detected the lingering tell-tale cigarette smoke and asked Albert what he had done that day. He tried his best to cover it up, but she was persistent and it was not long until the whole truth came out. The look of disappointment in her eyes along with the diaper story broke his heart and he promised never to smoke another cigarette. It was a vow that he kept.

One day the boys came home from school with a new word they had learned: "tuition." They had overheard classmates discussing what it cost their parents to send them to church school. As far as the boys knew their mother never set aside money for tuition. That evening they talked with their mother about it. Liese wondered why no one had told her about "tuition" when she had the boys register in the fall. When she had a chance to

Liese and her boys in Takoma Park (Christmas 1958).

talk to Mr. Neufeld, she asked him "Bruder Neufeld, was ist das tuition fuer die Schule?" ("Brother Neufeld, what is this tuition for the school?")

"Schwester Konrad, sie brauchen sich keine sorgen machen." ("Sister Konrad, you don't need to worry about that.") But Liese insisted on knowing, so he finally told her that, with his partner, Mr. Lutz, they had been covering the boys' tuition.

Liese and the boys were deeply grateful for the help they had received. However, their goal was to be self-supporting. By hard work and disciplined frugality, the day arrived when they could tell their benefactors that they were now able to pay the tuition themselves, and that they could help somebody else. The Neufeld and Lutz families had the mindset that when God blessed you with more than your needs, you aided others.

For several Christmases Liese and the boys were able to ride with the Neufeld family on their annual trip to Takoma Park, Maryland to visit Jeans' family. The trip allowed them to be with Willy and all the other members of Liese's family that had settled in the area. Eddie's sister, Theresa, who had lived for some time with Eddie and Liese back in Ukraine, took a special interest in her nephews and always gave them presents. Such gifts included items that the boys might want but could never afford.

On one of the Christmas trips, their Tante Theresa gave each of the boys a special gift that she had picked out for them. Albert was hoping that it would be a pair of Levi jeans. On the cusp of being a teenager he knew that all the cool guys wore Levi jeans held in place with a skinny belt with the buckle worn to the side. Their mom always bought jeans that were on sale and recommended by her friend Mr. Klopman, who owned the local dry goods store. He always had a special deal for her since he knew what she was attempting to accomplish in raising two sons on her own. Not only were the jeans off brand but also slightly irregular. You could not immediately see the problem but the boys knew it was there.

The fashion problem was doubly difficult for Albert as he usually got to wear the clothes that Karl outgrew and were still presentable. All he wanted for Christmas was his own pair of Levi's. No "hand-me-downs." No irregulars. No minor brand of "Huskies" jeans. Just Levi's. He didn't need a skinny belt to wear with the jeans for he already had one of those. They were cheap and easy to get.

Tante Theresa usually took the boys shopping to the Hecht Company Store in Silver Spring to buy their gifts, but this time there was no trip. In fact, they could not find any gifts with their names on them in the gift pile. Albert tried to be stoic but prayed as only a young would-be-teenager could for God to hear him and somehow, someway provide a pair of Levi jeans. When it came time to distribute the gifts Tante Theresa brought out the gifts for Karl and Albert. Immediately Albert realized that the package was too small for it to contain Levi's. It was a round object that looked like nothing that he might want or need. As he tore off the wrapping he saw that it was a bank in shape of a world globe.

Unobtrusively he shook it to see if it contained money, but heard nothing. Having always been taught to be polite, he thanked his aunt for the gift and told her that he would be able to use it in his studies. With a smile, she told him to check out the inside of the bank. Albert removed the bottom that held the money inside, glanced inside, but saw nothing. He looked puzzled but Tante Theresa said to check it out. Again slowly he stuck his index finger in the bank to discover a paper bill. Thinking it might be a dollar or two he pulled it out, only to discover that it was a $20.00 bill. In a strange way, God had answered his prayer, for the gift was more than enough to purchase two pairs of "honest-to-goodness" regular Levi Jeans.

During his elementary school years Albert had a second home with the family of his best friend, John Matthews, who lived just a block away. His dad was a tool and die machinist and worked for various auto related companies in the area. His mother was a stay at home mom who watched over Albert and John as they played together. The family often took Albert along with them on their vacation excursions to various sites and parks around the Detroit-Pontiac-Flint corridor. Karl became best friends with Royce Spalding whose dad was a truck driver and his mother taught at Adelphian Academy. He also

Liese and her boys in the backyard of the rented apartment (1960).

became friends with Jerry Bruckner when his dad came to work at the Academy furniture mill. It brought relief to Liese to have her boys looked after when she worked long hours from home. Despite that, the evening meal was always a time for her and her sons to share the day's activities as well as to pool any money that they had earned that day. The kitchen table became the place that continually brought them all together.

Chapter Eleven
Liese's Boys Becoming Men

Once the boys completed their elementary education they each spent a summer working on Adelphian Academy's farm earning enough money for the entrance fee. In the fall of his freshman year Karl obtained a job at a neighbor's family grocery store, the OK Super Market, cleaning up and stocking shelves. It provided employment and tuition money for his high school education. Albert spent an extra summer on the Academy farm and doubled up on lawn care, snow removal, and selling bread until Karl left for college and he took over the position at the grocery store. Although Albert worked as many hours as the management let him, they were always scheduled around his classes. Karl at college also worked extra hours. Since the school credited his pay to his school bill, he couldn't send money home, and the full burden of maintaining the home front depended on Liese and Albert.

After having her sons set aside tithe and offering from the money they earned, Liese had them keep a small amount that they could spend as they wished. Some determined saving enabled her to purchase an Emerson record player and several of the red vinyl Chapel records to play during Sabbath hours. Karl had done some saving of his own and decided to buy a record of one of the latest hit songs playing on various AM radio stations. Bringing it home, he got Liese and Albert together but would not let them see the record until they could hear it played. The record he purchased was "TRANSFUSION" written and performed by Jimmy Drake using the performance name of Nervous Norvus. The lyrics told the story of a careless driver who (cheerfully) receives blood transfusions after each of his accidents.

The song began with belching muffler noises, screeching tires, breaking glass, and the words: "Tooling down the highway doing 79. I'm a twin pipe papa and I'm feeling fine. Hey man dig that, was that a red stop sign? (Scrreeech! BANG!! Smash!) Transfusion. Transfusion. I'm just a solid mess of contusions. Slip the blood to me Bud…Transfusion. Transfusion. Never, never, never gonna speed again…Barnyard drivers are found in two classes—line crowding hogs and speeding jackasses. So, remember to slow down today." (lyrics.wikia.com/wiki/Nervous Norvus). "Transfusion" was a Top 20 hit in 1956, reaching #13 on Billboard's Hot 100 Chart. Many radio stations banned the song.

Liese did not criticize Karl, but she didn't quite know what to make of this purchase. Albert thought it was neat. His estimation of just how cool his brother was went up a couple notches. She prayed about it, and at the first opportunity purchased her own "45" to share with the boys. As Karl had done, she called them together to listen to her purchase and ask what they thought. Placing the record on the platen of the record player, she turned it on and watched for her sons' reaction. As the turntable spun the record, they heard Elvis Presley singing his rendition of "Peace in the Valley." Neither Liese nor Karl and Albert remember how many more times "Transfusion" was played but Elvis's record could be heard most weekends as they listened to the record player.

Liese watched with growing interest the development of her sons. Both were active in Pathfinders, studied hard, and worked long hours while attending Adelphian Academy. Karl was studious and read prodigiously, his grades reflecting his intense interest in his classes. Teachers at the academy soon learned that while both came from the same family, that did not mean the two of them had the same dedication when it came to school. Eventually Karl ended up being in the top ten percent of his graduating class with physics his favorite subject. Although Albert passed everything, he ended up right in the academic middle of his class. While Karl had a bent for things scientific, Albert was more into history and debating. Karl also had a great facility for memorizing. The English professor, Edward Kopp, challenged the students to memorize Robert Frost's 1,400-word poem, "The Death of the Hired Man," for extra credit. Wanting those extra points to ensure an A in the class, Karl took up the challenge, memorized Frost's poem, and recited it in front of the class.

Professor Kopp kept his part of the bargain, and Karl received an "A" in the class for not only memorizing but reciting it to the class.

For Sabbath, Liese, though tired, always baked something special: bread, rolls, or "streusel kuchen," a yeast-raised pastry with in-season-fruit (sliced apples, peaches, or plums) covered with crumbles. Sabbath afternoon would often have the table filled with the boys' friends chowing down, all the while discussing the adventures of the week and solving life's problems. Liese kept in the background listening, and at times adding an observation. It was her way of keeping up with what was happening and learning her sons' viewpoints. What she learned she used to good effect in dealing with situations arising between her and her sons, and felt well repaid for her efforts.

Karl graduated from academy in the spring 1959, knowing for sure that God had called him to work for Him in some capacity in the science area, most likely civil or aerodynamic engineering. He would make a lot of money, retire early, and raise prize dairy cattle. As a result, he enrolled at Emmanuel Missionary College (EMC) in Berrien Springs, Michigan. But during a Week of Prayer there, God spoke to him, suggesting that his plans were too self-serving. After much heart searching, prayer, and considering several options, he chose to become a science teacher. The decision gave him a sense of peace. Although he survived the Directed Teaching class, he concluded that secondary teaching was not his strength. Teaching at the college level required a graduate degree. How could he accomplish that? Finally, he decided to apply for acceptance at a university that would offer not only the necessary courses but also a teaching fellowship that would help pay the expenses.

Initially Albert wanted to become a medical doctor, but his studies at the high school level in chemistry, biology and physics convinced him that this was not where he would do well. While he passed all the courses he had no real desire to pursue those areas of study further. He was more than glad that he only had to take the basic science courses and not spend any more time in those subjects. Upon graduation, he knew that God had called him to study for the ministry. When he enrolled in college it was as a religious studies major.

At first Liese thought that the boys had it mixed up, because Karl was the more serious of the two boys while Albert tended to be more humorous and lighthearted. She believed that Karl should have been the preacher and Albert the teacher. But in the end, she concluded that God and the boys got it right in the choices they made and in the calls they received.

Even though Liese had a limited amount of education, she had taught herself to read and write in English. She could speak and correspond in German and Russian. Having absorbed her love of knowledge, it never occurred to either of her sons that they might not have enough money to go to college once they finished academy. They would work and study hard. That they owed to God and their mother. Their dad, were he with them, would want nothing but the best for them. For the boys, the possibility of their father still being alive and someday coming home from the war was a far distant thought. But for Liese it was an ever-present hope and reality. She never gave up hope of his return, and she wanted him to be proud of his family.

Willy and Gerhard sincerely did not believe that a single woman could effectively raise two boys, but she determined to raise her sons without the help of her brothers. They thought that Karl and Albert needed a father figure in their lives. They loved their sister dearly and sought only to help her. Willy had promised Eddie to watch over Liese and his boys in case he did not come back from the war, so on numerous occasions he invited Liese to move to Takoma Park and be closer to family. But happy in Holly, pleased with the direction in which the boys were growing, Liese stayed put.

Liese and Karl at Albert's Academy Graduation (1961).

When asked how she handled it all, she would often reply, "Well, I pray a lot." To her sons this seemed a strange answer. They weren't feeling rebellious, but worked and studied hard and had no desire to make life difficult for their mother. Why would she feel the need to "pray a lot"? Later, when Karl and Albert were raising their own families they often recalled their mother's remark and realized that parenting wisely required a lot of prayer.

Chapter Twelve

The Andrews University Years

Karl's graduation from Adelphian and his subsequent enrollment at Emmanuel Missionary College (now Andrews University) started a new era for the family. While attending Adelphian the boys were living at home and been considered "village students." They did not have to pay the boarding fees. EMC was located in the southwest corner of Michigan 200 miles from Holly. With Karl residing in Birch Hall, one of the men's dormitories, keeping up the home front was now fell to Liese and Albert. Then, when Albert graduated and started college he would have to live in the dormitory as well, placing the upkeep of home expenses on Liese alone. Her sons agreed that maintaining the home in Holly while they lived in the dormitory during the school year was too big a financial burden for their mother.

During Albert's senior year Karl initiated discussion of a possible move to western Michigan. "Mother, if you move to Berrien Springs we could live at home and save the residence and cafeteria expenses. The kind of work you are doing in Holly you can also do there." The boys had talked about it and thought perhaps she could even work at the college in one of their industries. Living costs were about the same in both places. When they first spoke to her about the possibility, Liese wasn't sure of the whole idea.

"You have thought things through," she told them, "but I have not, and I can't decide anything until I have prayed about making that kind of move and am clear that it is God's will. So, let me pray and think about it all."

Having established herself in Holly, she felt secure there. She realized that she would be unknown in Berrien Springs and a move there would require her to start over again. That prospect was daunting! Her sons gave her time and space and didn't press her for a decision.

Liese prayed and counseled with the Lutz's. Eventually she became comfortable with the idea, and when she made the financial comparisons, she realized that transferring to the college vicinity would be the wisest thing to do.

After academy graduation Albert spent the summer selling religious books near Lansing, Michigan. Karl arranged to move his mother and the household to an upstairs apartment just three blocks down the street from the EMC campus. Liese secured a job at the College Wood Products (CWP) where Karl worked. The plant manufactured wooden furniture such as student desks, beds, and dressers. The plant assigned Liese to the finishing department as a sander and she remained there for the next three years. The work was hard but it afforded her the opportunity to provide a home for her sons which allowed them to take a full academic load.

The money that each of the boys earned they never looked at as their own to do with as they pleased. Instead it all went into a common pot that paid for whatever expenses the family incurred. It had been the way of doing things that ensured that both Karl and Albert were able to graduate from Adelphian Academy. EMC always credited their campus earnings to their accounts, but they could have the tithe paid to Pioneer Memorial Church, the campus church.

Withdrawing cash from their accounts was difficult even when they were in positive territory because the next charges would push them into the negative. Whenever they had offers of cash jobs, they accepted and completed them immediately. That is how they could pay for incidentals and help with household expenses. Both completed their college studies in the normal four years. Each received a $100.00 alumni scholarship and graduated without debt.

A rusty but trusty black 1953 Studebaker joined the family when Albert graduated from academy in May of 1961. Over his mother's objection he had used his graduation gift money to buy the car to use in selling religious books during the summer. The car had a V-8 engine but with gas then 25 cents per gallon, no one worried about its mileage. Karl contributed dual glass pack mufflers which gave the car a powerful rumble. Karl's room-mate, Jared Bruckner, had also purchased an older Studebaker sedan and joined Albert in door-to-door canvassing. Neither Jerry nor Albert were great salesmen but both sold enough books to pay the necessary fees to begin the school year.

Later that fall evangelistic meetings were held in their sales area. A married couple attended faithfully and requested baptism. When asked, what had sparked their interest, they explained, "This past summer a young man came to our home selling religious books. He said his name was Albert Konrad. We bought the book, read it, and here we are." When told of the baptism, Albert realized that his summer of canvassing had been more successful than he could have imagined, reassuring him that his choice of a major was the right one.

While the book selling soon faded into just a memory, the '53 "Stude" became the family's main transportation. As the car continued to age it became rustier and less trusty. Both Karl and Albert signed up for Auto Shop classes at different times to get experience and a place to repair the car. The old car needed more work than either one anticipated. Frequent trips to local junkyards became a necessity to find the parts needed to keep it running. Those trips usually happened on Friday afternoon when neither of the boys worked or were in classes.

Albert soon learned what it meant to be a Theology major. One of their lab experiences involved participating in nearby evangelistic series. The evangelist was using a "Cathedral of the Air," a canvass dome inflated by a big air blower. The domes were somewhat of a novelty, but worked out quite well. The theology students took turns sleeping in the dome to keep an eye on things. When it came Albert's time, he asked Karl to go with him. At dusk, as they drove down the highway the latch on the hood gave way, and the hood popped up, completely obscuring Al's vision. Rolling down his window, Karl guided him to the side of the road. They secured the hood, continued on, and made it to the air dome just as the meeting ended. The night passed peacefully, so they left for home early in the morning. Breakfast, classes, and work were coming up fast.

The mishap with the hood gave it some serious dents that necessitated another trip to the junk yard. It seemed that the hood fiasco was just the beginning as the transmission began giving them trouble as well. With some diligent searching they found a transmission and the proper hood—in the right color, no less. In short order they had the parts installed and adjusted, and the "Stude" was ready for further adventures.

The fall of 1962 was the start of Karl's senior year. He would be graduating in May 1963, getting married in August, and beginning graduate school in September. Liese realized that her work in raising the boys was in its last phase. If they were to do a final family activity, it would have to take place during the Thanksgiving break or not at all. So, they made plans for a road trip to Takoma Park to visit the east coast relatives. After spending a lot of time and energy working on it, the car was running reasonably well. In their youthful exuberance, the boys concluded that they and the Studebaker were ready for the trip. Mom sat in the back praying for their safety and making sandwiches for the boys to eat. Karl and Albert alternated driving.

They had chosen the turnpike route: Indiana Tollway to the Ohio Turnpike to Pennsylvania Turnpike. While going through the Pennsylvania mountains, foggy weather slowed them down while the big semis passed them continually. Albert watched the semi-trailer lights disappear in the fog and announced, "I'm going to follow the next semi that passes us and keep his tail lights in view. From their height, they can see better than I can. That's why they can go faster." The next semi had just passed, and Al stepped on it. The engine revved, with mufflers barking, and the car accelerated. He kept those trailer lights in the center of his field of vision. After about an hour the fog began to lift and signs for their exit appeared. Heading southeast into Maryland, they made it safely to their destination.

Everybody was happy to see them. Cousin Hilda and husband, Alfred, had come from Philadelphia, and a lot of happy visiting took up the evening. The next morning everybody had a good look at the car. When Hilda saw, it she exclaimed "Tante Liese weren't you afraid to get in that rattle-trap?"

Feeling defensive about her sons, Liese replied, "Well, we did get here safely didn't we?" Karl and Albert assured their cousin that they had gone over the car before they started the trip. Somewhat mollified, Hilda didn't say anymore. But the relatives were still concerned about the condition of the car to the point that they made a proposition. They offered their extra car, a light green,1953 Plymouth four-door sedan that looked respectable and would be a safer ride for Hilda's favorite Aunt. The boys would have to figure out how to get the car from Philadelphia to Berrien Springs.

All too soon Sunday arrived and it was time to head back to Michigan. Driving conditions were much better, the car ran well, and the trip home was uneventful. During spring break Albert and a friend, who owned a VW, went to pick up the Plymouth in Philadelphia and bring it to Berrien Springs. The brothers decided to sell the Studebaker, and put a "For Sale" sign on it. A woman looking for some inexpensive transportation saw it and expressed an interest. After having the car's idiosyncrasies explained to her, she offered them $75.00. Albert accepted, since, after all, the car had initially cost $100.00 and had served them well. The Plymouth provided reliable transportation for the next two years. Trading it in on a 1961 Pontiac, Albert used the newer car while attending the Seminary and driving to various preaching appointments in the Chicago area.

Liese believed that God's leading had brought their family to America. She appreciated all the opportunities afforded to her sons. Though she never became well-to-do financially, she was always willing to pay her fair share of taxes and give back to God His tithe and offerings for the local church. One day when Albert was visiting he complained about how high his taxes had been the previous year. His mother just looked at him and said, "Remember Albert, in Russia they took it all. So just consider your blessings and pay your fair share joyfully."

A fervent believer in the Bible and its promises to those who are faithful stewards, she daily claimed the promise of Malachi: "Bring the whole tithe into the storehouse…Test me," says the Lord Almighty, "and see if I will not throw open the floodgates of heaven and pour out so much blessing that there will not be room enough to store it." (Malachi 3:10, NIRV)

Her faith would be severely tested, however. At the end of 1962 she and her sons had received their W-2 forms. Karl was anxious to file their taxes as quickly as possible so that whatever refund came to them could be applied to the tuition bill. In the rush to get it all done and mailed, Liese's forgot to sign her 1040 form. Because of the lack of a signature, the local IRS office pulled it and audited it. She had claimed both boys as dependents and since her earnings were not that high, the auditor could not see how she could provide support for both since that year the combined earnings for all three came right close to $3,000. The IRS would not allow the exemptions. It redid the calculations, and now instead of getting a refund she owed taxes. After she met with the auditor, he understood better what her financial condition was and what she attempting to do. With a kind heart, he made arrangements to take the extra tax from future refunds. Both boys received their refunds and used them for the semester expenses.

As her sons progressed in their college studies, Liese knew that soon both would be out on their own. That would be a huge change. How would she adjust? Karl completed his Bachelor's degree and graduated in May, 1963. The oldest and the first to leave the nest, he would move out in August. He had applied to and been accepted into the graduate chemistry program at Illinois Institute of Technology in Chicago, Illinois. A Teaching Assistantship would cover his expenses. That summer he worked for a local builder, helped Liese with the household expenses, saved money, and bought a car. Wouldn't you know, it was a 1953 Studebaker coupe that had been well cared for by its former owner, an elderly woman.

Karl was to marry his college sweetheart, Esther Anderson, a Minnesota girl, August 18. They would be living in Hinsdale, Illinois, where she was completing her Diploma RN program at the Hinsdale Sanitarium and Hospital School of Nursing. Since Esther would be marrying before completing the nursing program, she had to obtain permission from the nursing faculty to do so. By agreeing to work at the "San" after graduation, the hospital administration allowed them to rent an efficiency apartment in the nursing staff residence building. With everything set, the wedding took place. That September Karl started graduate classes and Esther completed the nursing program in November.

That fall, Albert's longtime Holly buddy, John Matthews, moved in and Liese again had two boys to look after, which eased the family breakup. John would transfer back to the dorm after Albert graduated. After they left, Liese continued to open her home to the children she had babysat in Holly. They found her place their second home, where they could enjoy both the food and the love dispensed there.

During his senior year Albert received a Ministerial Internship appointment from the Illinois Conference of Seventh-day Adventists. He graduated from the theology program in May, 1965, traded the faithful Plymouth in on a 1961 Pontiac Catalina, and married his academy sweetheart, Johnna Sue Mason. That summer he spent assisting one of the pastors in the Chicago area while Sue continued with her Hinsdale nursing program.

In the fall Albert moved back to Berrien Springs and found an apartment close to the Seminary for Sue and him. She completed the nursing program later that fall and started to work in a nearby hospital. Albert's internship included financial support for the completion of a Master of Arts degree at the university. He chose to major in Old Testament Studies. Although now alone at home, Liese still had one of her sons nearby. Often while Sue was working, Albert would pick Liese up from work, have lunch with her then take her back and head for the library for further study. After completing all his class work by the end of the 1966 summer session, Albert and Sue moved, and he began his ministerial work in south-central Illinois in September. Passing his comprehensive exams later that year, he graduated from Andrews in 1967.

Chapter Thirteen
Liese Becomes Oma

With both sons married and out on their own, Liese realized that her big task was done. With God's continual blessings, she had raised her boys. She wondered what God had in mind for her now. But she knew in her heart that He did have a plan for her life. Thinking of all she had been through, she knew that He had. Step by step, through the remainder of her life, she continued to discover His will.

> *With God's continual blessings, she had raised her boys. She wondered what God had in mind for her now.*

Shortly after Karl graduated, Andrews University completed construction of a new men's residence (Meir Hall). Liese applied for a position as housekeeper and was hired. She would be responsible for keeping the guest rooms, lounge areas, and hallways cleaned. Finally she had found a job that was not too strenuous for her and which she truly enjoyed, since cleaning was her most favorite type of work.

While cleaning in the dorm, she often found opportunity to talk with the young men living there, many of whom were homesick and needed a sympathetic ear. Through the years she had learned to deal with boys and knew how to listen and not criticize or laugh at some of the rather outlandish statements they made or the wild ideas they expressed. For many of the young men she filled the void of family. Often when they saw her carrying her vacuum or cleaning supplies to the next floor, they would take her load and have it up the stairs in a jiffy. Then they would call back to her "It's already up here."

Liese in her apartment. Berrien Springs, Michigan (1978).

The university administration hired three mature women to do the custodial work in Meier Hall. Liese's boss, while appreciating her hard work, was envious of her ability to connect with the young men. She often made things difficult for her and complained to the Dean that Liese was spending too much time talking and not enough time actually cleaning. When he would check he always found her tasks all done and her assigned areas immaculately clean. But the supervisor's criticism never let up, and finally when Liese turned 62 and was eligible for Social Security, she decided to retire. She never disclosed to the Dean the real reason for her retirement. Just avoiding her former boss, she kept herself busy doing other things.

Her former supervisor continued at the dorm until her negative attitude and inability to get along with whoever was hired to work led to her termination. It didn't take long until her relationship with friends and family also soured. One cold and rainy fall day, she found herself all alone and needed somewhere to go and be with someone who had a sympathetic ear. She decided to visit Liese and knocked on her door. When Liese saw her standing on her doorstep, disheveled, cold, and wet, she immediately invited her inside. As the woman poured out her tale of misery and woe, Liese's heart went out to her. After a warm meal and good visit, she was invited to come back anytime, and she did return often. Through God's grace and Liese's caring heart the onetime antagonist became a friend.

When Liese retired, her initial monthly Social Security check was just $94.40 though she also received a small stipend from the German Government as a result of Eddie's MIA status.

Together they comprised her base income for the next nine years. She was able to supplement this amount by sitting with the elderly parents of various Andrews faculty and administrators, and cleaning at the local Adventist Book Center. In her retirement she found the time to can many of the vegetable and fruits that abounded in the area. She was given bruised or misshapen peaches, plums, apples, and tomatoes that she patiently trimmed and prepared for canning. Often she would share the bounties of her work with the boys and their growing families when they came to visit.

God's floodgates of blessing were not about financial riches for Liese and the boys. But blessings were bestowed since both sons graduated from college and graduate school without debt. The tough conditions of her earlier years had taught her how to be careful with her money and no matter what the circumstances to save something. Though Liese was never rich in earthly goods, at the time of her passing she had accumulated enough savings so that the family could promptly pay her medical and burial expenses. Enough money remained for a small inheritance for each of her sons. God had kept his promise!

Liese became good friends with several older, single women. Contacting each other regularly to see if everything was okay, they would share encouraging thoughts gleaned from their individual study and get together for visits and trips to the grocery store. She was happy with her life even though Albert moved to Illinois (and later to New York City), and Karl to Texas. While she enjoyed visiting her sons and their families and having them visit her, she was content to live in Berrien Springs. In fact, when Karl and Esther built a house with an attached double car garage, had it insulated and the rough plumbing put into the floor and wall so that it would be ready to convert into an efficiency apartment, she was in no hurry for the move to Texas.

The arrival of grandchildren was another development that gave renewed meaning and purpose. Happily, Liese assumed the role of "Oma" ("grandma"). Eventually, she had seven grandkids: two from Albert and Sue, Anni (October, 1966) and John (July, 1969); and five from Karl and

Esther, Krista (January, 1967), Paul (January, 1970), Ellie (December, 1971), Karl (October, 1973), and Monica (February, 1977).

Through the years Liese loved telling them all the family stories, teaching the girls how to crochet, and fixing some of the favorite family dishes. When Albert experienced a series of medical problems with his back and had to leave the active ministry, she came to New York for several months to care for him and watch Anni and John. Before she passed away she was able to get to know all her grandchildren from the oldest, Anni, at age 15, to the youngest, Monica, at age 4. They all can still recall stories that Oma shared especially with them.

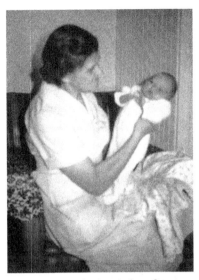

Liese with Anni, her first grandchild in October 1966.

Chapter Fourteen
The Letter

The January 1966 winter was in full swing with snow piled high on both sides of the street. Karl had just graduated with his Master of Science in Physical Chemistry degree and was cleared for study toward the PhD at Illinois Institute of Technology. His brother was completing his Master of Arts degree in Old Testament Studies at Andrews University's Theological Seminary.

Albert's classes and study time took up his mornings. Often when Sue was working and it was noon he would head for the dorm, pick up his mother, drive to her apartment, get the mail, and have lunch with her. More snow had fallen the night before and on that Wednesday the plowing had piled it so high that it almost blocked the row of mailboxes. With careful maneuvering Albert got the car close enough for Liese to reach the mailbox and retrieve the mail. As she brought the various envelopes inside the car window, she began to tremble and tears welled up in her eyes. In her hand was an official looking letter from the German Red Cross.

Tearing open the envelope she read out loud. "Dear Mrs. Konrad. We have recently received correspondence from an Eduard Konrad who is looking for his family. His wife's name is Elizabeth Hann Konrad and the boys are named Karl and Albert. We were able to locate your current address. Please let us know if you are that family. We will then forward his current address." The letter went on to give the birth dates of Liese, Karl, and Albert as well as their last address in Lask at the time he had to report for duty on January 15, 1945.

Twenty-one years had passed! Now this was the first indication that Eddie was alive! It made it difficult to focus on lunch that day. When Albert called Karl that evening, the news, took his brother's breath away. The telephone was busy as Liese shared it with relatives and friends.

The letter from the Red Cross was dated Monday, January 24, and received by Liese on January 26. And by Friday, January 28, Liese had one of her friends help her to compose the formal response. The letter stated that she and sons were thrilled that Eduard was still alive and searching for his family. "Yes," she wrote, "the information fits exactly. All the individuals that he mentions are alive and well. All of these 21 years we have waited and sought to find him. We wondered what had happened with him and thank God that he is alive. Our earnest wish is that soon he will be with us."

Wednesday, February 4, another Red Cross letter arrived giving Eddie's address and informing Liese that they passed on the information she had supplied. Eddie's address took away some of the joy. He was alive, but was still in the Soviet Union, living in Arkhangelsk (Archangel). This port city lies on both banks of the Northern Dvina River near its exit into the Barents Sea (White Sea) in far northwest European Russia. She realized there would be huge barriers to surmount before they could ever see him.

It took some weeks before Liese received a letter from Eddie. It confirmed that he was alive but broke her heart. It was the second letter that he had written but for unknown reasons it arrived first. She was not prepared for its content! Eddie explained that he had been told that Liese and the boys had perished in the Russian Army's attack on Lask. Never permitted to leave the Soviet Union, he had married again. Now he had a second family consisting of his wife, Paulina, a son, Constantine, and daughter, Elena.

Then he explained how he had come to start his search for her and the boys. One day he heard that a German freighter was in port and that one of the sailors was named Konrad.

Although he tried his best to make contact, the ship had already left. All the old emotions began to stir. Maybe just maybe, Liese and the boys had somehow survived. He determined to write to the German Red Cross. Amazingly, the authorities allowed his letter to go through. Now he knew. They were alive!

The letter was apologetic and honest, but its contents were an emotional and physical hit that devastated Liese. Her commitment and love for Eddie had always been strong. Even after receiving the MIA letter from the German Government, she could not bring herself to consider marriage and never sought another man's companionship. She could not, for in her heart she believed that Eddie was still alive and would someday come home. Furthermore, she was doubly afraid that if she married another man he might not or could not love her boys as much as she did. Would he treat them as her Eddie would if he were with them? She remembered the difficulties he had in relating to his stepfather.

In her heart, she was sure that Eddie would also wait for her no matter what. Their love had been providential and the boys a gift from God. Their family was meant to be forever, or at least for this world. So, when the letter came with news that he had married another woman, the hurt was not only emotional but physical. Albert's wife, Sue, was an RN and recognized that the stress was too much for her mother-in-law. Sue called a physician she knew well and asked him to prescribe a sedative for Liese. Somehow, she managed to keep on going with the activities of life.

Liese was not one to harbor bitterness or resentment. As time passed she forgave Eddie and came to terms with what the realities that time, war, imprisonment, and separation had caused. Also she worked hard with her sons so that they would not harbor resentment about the situation.

Eddie had retained his fluency in German and a regular correspondence ensued between him and Liese, Karl, Willy, Alma and Therese. Albert could speak German and read its printed form but had difficulty with cursive German writing. In a limited way, he could correspond with his father several times a year. In his letters, Eddie expressed an intense longing once again to see Liese and his two boys.

Karl and Albert determined to do their best to fulfill his desire. It had required the utmost frugality and firm determination to take on every job that opened for them to complete their undergraduate education. Now, with both in school and their income limited, they moved slowly but steadily forward on a seemingly impossible dream. They undertook the mission not only because they wanted to see their dad but because Liese encouraged them. The relatives promised to help financially if visitation plans did actually materialize. The biggest hurdle to a visit was getting an exit visa for Eddie. The process was lengthy and arduous and began with a Vusov, (a letter in Russian) from the family inviting Eddie for a visit and guaranteeing to meet all his expenses. The letter had to be certified by a local Notary Public, the Notary Public certified by the county clerk, the county clerk certified by the Michigan Secretary of State, who then had to be certified by the US Department of State. At the end of this process the document, decorated with seals and ribbons attesting its authenticity, was quite impressive and was sent to Eddie.

After receiving the Vusov, Eddie applied for an exit visa. The local area government agency had to give an account to higher authorities for every exit permit granted, but not for a denial. Since neither Liese's family nor Eddie had political influence, they faced a discouraging series of rejections and everyone had to be satisfied with letters and pictures.

Eddie wrote of his life. Although released from the gulag in 1955, he still had to stay in the Archangel area. His tailoring skills got him a job in a garment factory. When the management discovered his mechanical abilities, it gave him the responsibility for the maintenance and repair of the sewing machines. He also compiled a list of clients for whom he did custom tailoring. The extra income made for an easier life, one more comfortable for the family. The two children were healthy and growing. They had lodging and enough food. During the short summers, they would gather and dry mushrooms and berries and catch fish in the Dvina River.

Karl heard about a Chicago company that guaranteed the delivery of packages sent to the USSR. They supplied the list of acceptable items along with the amount of import duty and taxes for each. After the family prepaid the duties, taxes, and the company's fee and brought the items, the company would pack them up and ship them. Willy, Alma, and Theresa sent Karl money and a list was made. It included a quality leather Soccer ball and pump for Constantin and stylish tights for Elena, and Liese included several nice, embroidered tea towels for Paulina.

In one of his letters Eddie stated that quality clothing was expensive. Karl went to Chicago's Maxwell Street and, entering one of the many custom tailoring shops, asked for advice in choosing all the materials needed for a quality suit. When told the reason for the request, the shop owner displayed several samples of his nicest English worsted wool textiles. After Karl chose a distinguished looking color, the man got all the other needed materials together—lining, buttons, pockets, shoulder pads, zipper, and thread—and quoted a decent price for the lot. This was put in the package for Eddie with the idea that he would make the suit and sell it for a good profit.

It took some time for the package to make its way from Chicago to Archangel, but Eddie stated in one of his letters to Karl that they had received everything. They were thankful to be remembered, the children enjoyed their gifts, and Paulina was especially touched that Liese had thought of her. Eddie never said anything directly about what he did with the suit material, but reading between the lines of what he actually wrote let everyone know that it resulted in good things for the family.

Over the years Liese and her brothers and sisters, working with relatives in Germany, were able to obtain addresses and make contact with relatives still in the Soviet Union. Theresa even got the address of her long-lost sister, Rosalia, who was living in Moscow and was married to a Seventh-day Adventist minister. They shared the addresses with Eddie. No longer did he feel so alone, and the contacts eased the loneliness and pain of not being able to see Liese and his grown sons. Eddie lost no time writing to Rosalia. At first she did not want to respond, however as she thought about her past, long forgotten memories came back, and she answered. He went to see her. What a reunion! At their separation, he thought that he had lost her forever. He could never forget her cries. Now she was all grown up, married, and a mother herself. They had so many experiences to share. How spiritually awakening and reassuring it was to be with her again.

Rosalia and her minister husband were committed and active believers. With God's protection, they had survived the years of Stalin's terror, the rigors of the war, and the anti-religious campaigns of the Soviet government. While not allowed the privileges of higher education—university enrollments were reserved for Komsomol members (communist youth organization members)—they were cheerful and happy. Eddie yearned for the assurance and trust with which Rosalia and her husband faced the challenges and disappointments of life.

> *Eddie yearned for the assurance and trust with which Rosalia and her husband faced the challenges and disappointments of life.*

Eddie's mind went back to January, 1945. Although granted a greatly-needed furlough, the time spent with Liese and the children had been much too short. He had worked hard to gather wood, coal, and food staples to see Liese and the boys through the winter. Long discussions with Willy clarified his spiritual questions, and he had committed his life to God. Now he felt ready for baptism. Willy assured him that God understood his situation and accepted his commitment even though it was impossible to carry out the actual rite of baptism.

Then came the summons to return to his translator unit and report to headquarters by January 15, 1945. Despite the harsh winter the Red Army had advanced faster and farther than anticipated. He had to go. One last time he hugged Liese and the boys. At the door, he prayed "Oh God, please watch over my family." With a short but loving "Auf Wiedersehen" he was out the door and gone. It was the last time he had any contact with them! Twenty-one years had passed. Then that letter from the German Red Cross. Somehow Liese and the boys had survived and were now living in America. God had heard his prayer!

Eddie and his sister Rosalie (1978).

Chapter Fifteen

Eddie's Journey and Captivity

For Liese and the boys their journey ended in freedom. Eddie was not so fortunate. His call back to active duty on January 15, 1945 was a prelude to disaster. Nothing the German Army did kept the Russians from advancing from the east and the Allies from the west, the south or the north. The German leadership declared Posen (Poznan in Polish) a fortress point, and the German Army sought to make a determined stand there. Posen lay in the western part of Poland that Nazi Germany had annexed following its invasion of the country in 1939.

But the Red Army had other plans, and in mid-January of 1945 they launched a massive assault on the German Army's garrison. Their objective was the elimination and surrender of the forces stationed there. The defeat of the garrison took an entire month of painstaking and intense urban combat. The final assault on the city's citadel by the Red Army resulted in the death and capture of thousands.

During this last stand, Eddie had met another Regular German Army soldier named Peter Epp, who served with him in the same interpreter company in Posen. We have based Eddie's story of his capture and captivity on recollections shared in a letter that Peter wrote to Liese a few years prior to her death.

Eddie and Peter were assigned to a company of 15 soldiers who were given orders to establish an outpost about three miles from Posen. His

Commanding officer ordered Eddie to dig a foxhole and occupy it along with another soldier. Curiosity about his foxhole-buddy led Eddie to tell him who he was. "I am a Russian-German from Khortitza and my name is Eddie Konrad." His new-found friend looked stunned as Eddie talked.

"Man! Can you believe it? I'm from Yazekovo, which is only 25 kilometers from Khortitza and my name is Peter Epp." For Eddie and Peter, it was as if two brothers had found each other! They promised to stick together and keep track of each another no matter what would happen.

During the month-long siege Eddie was assigned messenger duty. While Peter had to stay in the fox hole in preparation for the coming battle, Eddie had to pass on messages from headquarters to the various soldiers scattered over the area. His missions were extremely dangerous. Whole artillery batteries would open fire whenever the enemy spotted a messenger. More than 5,000 German troops died in the month-long siege, but the Red Army sustained the loss of more than 12,000 of its soldiers. God seemed to protect Eddie when the bombs exploded around him, and he survived that month-long encirclement without being wounded.

During the night of February 14, all the fox-hole soldiers received orders to break through the Russian encirclement and attempt to regroup with German units farther west. Eddie's messenger duties had kept him moving all over the area, and he had lost track of his friend Peter. By that time the Red Army had advanced as far west as the Oder river and the only option the soldiers had was to attempt a breakout. As the men organized into small groups, Eddie saw Peter and called out to him. Again, they determined not to get separated. Their group managed to get through the encirclement without injury, but the retreat became a disorganized rout.

Within three days Eddie and Peter were part of a small group hiding in the forest during the day and trying to slip westward during the night. It consisted of an SS officer and seven SS soldiers along with Eddie and Peter who were regular Wehrmacht troops. The SS officer made it clear that no one was to surrender but must fight to the last drop of blood. No love existed between the SS and the Wehrmacht, so Eddie and Peter did not pay attention to the officer's wild commands. Wehrmacht soldiers, not SS troopers, they were unwilling to die needlessly. Their goal was to survive and find their families. They determined to ditch the group at the first opportunity and did so.

In the gray early morning light, peering through the fog, they could just make out a farm in the distance and headed for it. They had not had anything to eat for three days and hoped to find something at the farmhouse. Slowly and carefully, they crawled on their stomachs, checking things out. Not seeing any signs of life, they approached the house. The farm had been abandoned. There were no people, no animals, no food!

They decided to crawl into the barn, cover up with hay and at least get some sleep during daylight before continuing westward in the night. But before falling asleep a loud voice commanded "German soldiers come out with your hands up!" Looking out through a crack in the door they saw that armed Polish policemen surrounded the barn. Their only option was to comply with the order.

Any hope of getting to their wives and children dashed, the war, for them, was over, their future uncertain! It would no longer be freedom that awaited them but death at worst or prison at best.

Remembering his pastor father and faith-believing wife, Eddie in his heart cried out to God, and a peaceful assurance came over them. The Polish Police took them to the police station. The police chief who could speak German initially interrogated them. A good man, he did not mistreat them. He simply sought to gain the necessary information to log their capture.

After discerning that they had not had anything to eat for several days, he immediately ordered that they receive something to eat. Since Eddie and Peter were soldiers and not civilians the police had no choice but to take them to the Russian officer in charge of the area. The police chief's last words to them were, "I am sorry. I cannot keep you here. Your situation is going to be grim. May God, help you." Then the police led them away to the Russian Army command post.

Once in the custody of the Red Army everything changed. Immediately the soldiers treated them not only as if they were POW's but as if they had committed treason for they had been born in Russia and had joined the German Army. The interrogators used their truncheons freely and beat them severely. The German armed forces had not been gentle with the prisoners they had captured, and now their captors were squaring accounts.

After the initial beating and a short interrogation, the Russians sent them back to Posen to a POW camp. For some unknown reason, after just three days in the POW camp, Eddie and Peter found themselves transferred to a Polish prison. There the treatment was better and hope for a possible future began again. *Surely,* Eddie thought, *My Liese is praying for me because God is watching over us.* The move spared them the worst treatment. Eddie had heard that two of the captured German officers at that POW camp had been beaten to death and the rest tortured.

Six weeks later they were transported to northwestern Russia's Archangel district to build a railroad. The camp commandant chose Eddie to be his translator since most of the prisoners were Germans from the Posen, East Prussia, and Pomeranian areas. Because of his translator position Eddie had it better than Peter and would smuggle extra rations to him whenever he could.

Eddie was glad that he had found a real friend in Peter and that they could be in the same camp. During evenings and nights, they had to endure interrogation. Because they were housed among internees, they hoped that the Russian Authorities would consider them as internees, since they had been granted German citizenship. But after three months the camp administration separated all inmates born in Russian territories and sent them to a special prison for political offenders in Archangel. Again, Eddie felt that God was answering Liese's continuing prayers, because he ended up in the same ward as Peter.

Eddie and Peter agreed to act as if they not known each other and that recent circumstances had brought them together. If Eddie's status as a German Wehrmacht translator became known, it would be very difficult for him. After several days, the camp administration separated them and intense interrogation began. The separation was intended to prevent them from talking to each other and comparing their treatment. The interrogation lasted from August 25, 1945 until January 25, 1946. It was a very difficult time. The daily schedule was unrelenting. It began with lights on at 6:00 a.m., then continuous questioning without rest or sleep for remainder of the day. Lights were turned off at 11:00 p.m. and on again at midnight. More interrogation until 4:00 a.m. Finally, the lights came on again at 6:00 a.m. to resume the vicious cycle.

After completion of the interrogation process, Eddie found himself back with Peter in the initial ward to which the camp had assigned them. Next, they were transferred to a regular prison where they would be housed until their trial. While the wait for the trial lasted more than a year, the actual trial was short and the sentence imposed swift. Peter was found guilty and sentenced to ten years of hard labor in a gulag. He served out his whole time working in that lumber camp. Finally released, Peter reunited with his wife and children who had not been able to escape from Ukraine when Liese and her family had left in 1943. Eventually Peter and his family were given permission to leave and make their way to Germany and freedom.

Eddie's trial resulted in the same 10-year sentence as his friend Peter Epp had received. Initially the authorities sent him to an invalid gulag nearby and then transferred him to a prison near Archangel where he served out the remainder of his sentence.

Chapter Sixteen

The Final Homecoming

Eddie realized that his capture, the rough treatment, the 10-year sentence, the loss of Liese and the boys, the establishment of a second family, never meeting another Adventist believer during all those lonely years, had embittered him. He had to admit to himself that his commitment had gotten pushed into a long-forgotten corner of his heart and mind. The years after his release had kept him busy and occupied with just getting the necessary things of life done. Even when he had found that Liese and the boys were alive, circumstances prevented him from doing anything about it. It seemed that they were controlling him more than he did them. But time and the events in his life worked on his memories and his outlook. Glimpses of a loving God who was still able to control life began to become clearer and clearer to him.

Eddie and his family made a vacation trip to the old hometown of Khortitza where they visited with nephews Albert and Willy Kampen and their families. He remembered when they were drafted. As they shared experiences he saw that despite their Soviet captivity, Siberian imprisonment and constant harassment, they maintained their commitment and were active leaders in their churches. Also denied further education, they were working as common laborers. Finally, he had to admit to himself that with God's help he too could have kept his commitment. What to do? And how to do it? Rosalia was always encouraging, as were the nephews. But he had no Bible and no way to get one, and that made it very hard to come to a decision. The years moved on.

The people he worked with respected him, and his economic situation improved. He was on a five-day workweek and could afford a small used car. The children reached adulthood.

Paulina and Eddie's health became more and more precarious. She had been an overseer of supplies for her collective. When a widow and her family were in dire need, she had taken it upon herself to give her what she needed. But that initiative angered her superiors, who arrested, tried, and sentenced her to prison. By 1976 her health had deteriorated so badly that she died.

Again, Eddie was alone. After Paulina's death Eddie continued to work as his health allowed. By the summer of 1981 his heart could no longer sustain the pace of living required of him. It gave him so much trouble that he had to be hospitalized twice. But in the end, it was pneumonia, the "old man's friend," combined with his heart problems that finally brought his suffering to an end. One evening in July of 1981 Eddie went to bed as usual and during the night lapsed into a deep sleep and slipped into a peaceful and dignified end with little suffering. He had lived only 63 years of life and less than 7 of those were spent together with Liese.

Eddie realized that his capture, the rough treatment, the 10-year sentence, the loss of Liese and the boys, the establishment of a second family, never meeting another Adventist believer during all those lonely years, had embittered him.

With Eddie's death his letters to Liese came to a stop in the summer of 1981. At first she had no idea of the reason for the stoppage. But finally, news of his death began to dribble in from different relatives. Together their love had endured far too much for Liese simply to accept the news from a casual mention in a letter. She needed more. So, she requested official confirmation of the date and manner of his passing. After an excruciating passage of time the notice arrived in November from sources in the USSR that Eddie had died on July 14, 1981, 36 years since their separation from each other. Now with a stunning reality her wait for him was over.

When she shared the official notice with Karl and Albert, her sons sought to help her deal with the reality of it all. Karl called Albert and asked, "What can we do since we both live so far away?"

"How about we purchase flowers for the of front mom's church, Pioneer Memorial, located on the campus of Andrews University, in honor of dad's memory," Albert suggested. "I can call my sister-in-law and see if she will arrange for the flowers for this coming Sabbath." And on that Sabbath, the actuality of Eddie's death became all too real. Liese stood by the flowers and knew in her heart that her prayer had finally been answered and her Eddie had come home.

Once the news of Eddie's passing had been verified, Liese felt her life was now complete. She had lived through two World Wars, famines, a wedding, the death of a child, the birth of her sons, seeing them graduate from college, university and seminary. She had watched them each get married and had experienced her seven grandchildren.

Liese at Pioneer Memorial Church in early November 1981.

She knew that Eddie had also come home to the Father's heart from the words that he wrote in a letter dated October 19, 1980. "Everybody I know tells me to be hopeful and not give up. It is too soon for me to die. They remind me that I have loved ones that are waiting for me both for heaven and here on earth. So, I need to live. I am not ready to die and would like to live, but my conscience bothers me. I wonder if the dear Lord can forgive me for all that I have done? I am so far behind in spiritual matters. I can't seem to pray. The Bible is strange to me. In fact, I don't even have one because it is so difficult to get one. But what I have now I will not push away…I think about you and my family here with me. Trying to resolve the issues that have come about drive me to distraction. I don't know how it will all be resolved. But I have put my life in God's hand so if it is His will that I shall live, it will all be worked out."

Liese no longer waits for Eddie. He has come home. Hope has met reality. Faith has found fulfillment. She is at peace. As if prescient, early in 1981, Liese wrote a short statement of her faith in God. "I was born on July 7, 1910 in Khortitza, South-Central Ukraine. I was the 10th of eleven children. The most important step of my young life occurred in May of 1924 when I decided to become a baptized member of the Seventh-day Adventist Church. This decision was greatly influenced by the legacy I received from my parents, who themselves discovered the Great Advent Hope from the reading and study of their wedding gift Bible. In baptism, I surrendered my life to Jesus. I asked God to keep this Advent Hope alive in my life and to give me strength for each new day so that I might be a blessing to others. In the course of a long life one may experience a lot of trouble and sorrow. World War II did not spare me. As I reflect on my life, I have not regretted the decision I made and would not change it."

On a cold rainy Friday afternoon, November 20, 1981, Liese had a stroke and was rushed to the hospital. Even though she was in a coma Liese lived long enough for both of her sons to come to Berrien Springs and be with her as two days later she breathed her last. Karl and Albert arranged for her funeral to be held on Wednesday afternoon, November 25. Her brother Willy, her sisters-in-law, Alma and Theresa, and several of her nephews and nieces joined her sons on that day. It was a bittersweet day for both Karl and Albert as they had never known life without the love and prayers of their mother. Even though they were grown and had families of their own, they had kept regular contact with her, and she prayed for them daily.

At the funeral service, Karl and Albert spoke in honor of their mother. Albert read various scriptures including portions of Job 19:25-27: "But as for me, I know that my Redeemer lives, and he will stand upon the earth at last. And after my body has decayed, yet… I will see God! I will see him for myself. Yes, I will see him with my own eyes" (NLT). Revelation 21:1-4 says, "Then I saw a new heaven and a new earth, for the old heaven and the old earth had disappeared. And the sea was also gone… I heard a loud shout from the throne, saying…God's home is now among his people! He will live with them, and they will be his people. God himself will be with them. He will wipe every tear from their eyes, and there will be no more death or sorrow or crying or pain. All these things are gone forever" (NLT).

Karl spoke about her life journey and the faith and trust in God that had sustained her through it all. He concluded his eulogy with the words "The greatest legacy that our mother left us was the prayers that she prayed. Through prayer her faith sustained us. She raised us boys and kept true to her faith and now she sleeps and rests safe in the arms of Jesus. Albert and I know it was our mother's prayers that kept us safe and will guide us on our life journey."

The news of her death deeply saddened her brother Willy. He had promised Eddie, his best friend and brother-in-law, that he would always take care of Liese. While he had kept his promise, now as she lay in the casket, he felt his heart about to break. She looked so peaceful, more alive than dead. He wanted desperately to simply call out "Liese, Liese, please wake up!" However, he had no option but to accept the reality that she was gone. He knew that his sister was sleeping safely, resting in the loving arms of the God who had always guided their family.

All the relatives celebrated Liese's life by getting together for a Thanksgiving dinner hosted by Albert's sister-in-law, Emily Garrett. As they sat around the larger than usual dinner table they shared the stories of their journey from Ukraine to Poland to Germany and finally to America. The stories were so familiar but wonderful to hear again, stories that Liese had so often told the boys and their children. They thanked God for the memories and their mother's faith.

Once again Karl and Albert made arrangements for flowers to be placed in the front of Pioneer Memorial Church. This time it was in honor of their mother who loved so freely and so long, and who had died within a few weeks of receiving confirmation of her Eddie's death. Faith has found fulfilment. Eddie and Liese are at rest. Their love story awaits its culmination in eternity, awaiting His call on that resurrection morning. Until then their sons continue to remember their parent's love story and seek to live out the life lessons that Eddie and Liese taught them.

Epilogue

Karl and Albert have experienced joy and sorrow in their lives. Joy in that they were able to do the work that they loved for all their lives and have a good quality of health in their retirement. Tragedy and sorrow came to both as they each lost a son. The story that began in the nineteenth century continues into the twenty-first. Only time and eternity will reveal the ending.

Karl graduated from Andrews University in May 1963 with a BA, majoring in chemistry. That fall he began graduate work at the Illinois Institute of Technology in Chicago, completing both the MS (January 1966) and the PhD (January 1969) in physical chemistry, then joined the faculty of Southwestern Union College, now Southwestern Adventist University. For many years, he served as Chair of the Department of Mathematics, and Physical Sciences, and spent three years as Vice President for Academic Affairs. His wife, Esther, is a Registered Nurse (RN Diploma, Hinsdale Sanitarium and Hospital School of Nursing; 1963, BSN Southwestern Adventist University, 1993) and together they raised five children (Krista, Paul, Elizabeth, Karl, and Monica). All of the children have become established in their fields. Now he is Opa (Grandpa) and Esther is Grandma to 10 grandchildren (three boys and seven girls). He and Esther have both retired and continue to live near the University in Keene, Texas.

Albert received a Bachelor of Arts degree in Religion Studies in May of 1965 from Andrews University and a Master of Arts Degree in 1967.

Beginning his work as a pastor for the Illinois Conference of Seventh-day Adventists in September of 1966. He spent 20 years in the pastoral ministry in South-central Illinois, and in suburban churches of New York City and Washington, DC. Because of several health problems that resulted in four back surgeries, he took a permanent medical leave from the ministry in August 1989. He then became a Licensed Nursing Home Administrator and spent 20 years supervising various nursing home in Pennsylvania and Maryland. When he reached retirement age, his health permitted him to get back in the ministry, and he spent six more years as a pastor on the eastern shore of Maryland.

He and his wife, Sue, a Registered Nurse, raised two children, Anni and John. Both children became established in their field of study. Albert is Opa to three granddaughters and one great-grandson. Fully retired at the end of April 2016, he now lives close to Anni in the Shenandoah Valley of Virginia.

After Eddie died, the boys lost contact with their siblings, the language barrier being too great. Following the collapse of Communism, and Tante Theresa's retirement, she went to Russia to visit her sister, Rosalia, who was living in Moscow. The sisters then made a train trip visit to Eddie's daughter, Elena, her husband Valentin, and their four children living in Kazakhstan. That visit established contact with Elena but not with Constantin. Because Elena and Valentin were of German extraction, the authorities allowed them to immigrate to Germany during the 1990s. They settled near Wilhelmshaven, a coastal city in northern Germany.

In 2006 Karl, Albert, and Albert's son, John, participated in a Ukrainian mission trip sponsored by Southwestern Adventist University. The flight to and from Ukraine had a layover in Frankfurt, Germany. On the return flight, they extended their layover a few days, rented a car, and drove to Wilhelmshaven. It was Christmas day, Karl typed in their sister's address and left the car's navigation system language in German to put them in the right mood. Driving north the GPS directed them to the village of Friedeberg-Horsten and right to Elena's house. For the first time the boys were able greet and hug their sister. Karl told her that she had a strong resemblance to Albert. She told him, that he reminded her of her brother Constantin (who had died some years earlier in Russia).

In May 2013, Karl, Esther and Albert made another a journey to Germany. They visited with their cousin, Johann Kampen, in Augsburg and then traveled to nearby Salzburg, Austria, for sightseeing. After stopping in Wildenreuth to see old friends and renew memories, they drove north to Friedeberg-Horsten to visit Elena and Valentin and stayed several days.

They had a grand visit with their sister, her husband Valentin, and all of their nephews and nieces. With all of them fluent in German they communicate regularly.

Albert, Elena and Karl together during Christmas at her home
in the village of Friedeberg-Horsten 2006

Explanatory Map Notes

The purpose of this map (page 42) is to give geographic context to the long journey from Ukraine to Germany, and to clearly show all the areas that Liese, Eddie and the boys either lived in or traveled through. The locations of the villages, towns and cities indicated on the map are close approximations of their actual locations. Though the travel routes are drawn as strait lines, the real ones meandered since neither the railroad tracks nor the highways or back roads were direct ones.

Khortitza was the starting point of the journey. It still exists today but is now part of the larger city and area called Zaporozhe. The distance traveled by train from south-central Ukraine to north-western Poland is longer than 1,500 kilometers and took 11 days. It should have required only three days. The train did not have priority status, and was often sidelined for trains carrying troops and military supplies.

Preusisch-Stargard was the name given the area by the Germans during WW2. It is now part of Poland and the Polish name for the area is Gdansk-Starograd. The family was stationed here from October 1943 through June of 1944.

Lask was the name of the village to which the family was moved after the granting of their German citizenship. It was in Lask that Liese and boys saw Eddie for the last time, and from there began their horse drawn wagon trek to Germany in January 1945.

Wittenberg is where Willy had the wagon train pivot south and head toward Bavaria. The approximate distance traveled by the group from Lask to Wildenreuth was over 1,100 kilometers and took 2 ½ months.

Zhytomyr is where Eddie was born, and Poznan is where Eddie was stationed and finally captured by the Polish police and turned over to the Russians. The city is located to the north and east of Lask on the map. Archangel, located in the upper right-hand corner of the map by the White Sea, is the area and city where the Soviets imprisoned Eddie and later permitted him to live. Bremerhaven, while not listed on the map, was the port where Liese and the boys left for America in 1952. It is located north of the city of Bremen and west of Hamburg.

AB ASPECT Books

We invite you to view the complete
selection of titles we publish at:
www.ASPECTBooks.com

We encourage you to write us
with your thoughts about this,
or any other book we publish at:
info@ASPECTBooks.com

ASPECT Books' titles may be purchased in
bulk quantities for educational, fund-raising,
business, or promotional use.
bulksales@ASPECTBooks.com

Finally, if you are interested in seeing
your own book in print, please contact us at:
publishing@ASPECTBooks.com
We are happy to review your manuscript at no charge.

CPSIA information can be obtained
at www.ICGtesting.com
Printed in the USA
FSOW03n2114121017
39747FS